STolen from Dan

Five Alarm Leadership

FIVE ALARM LEADERSHIP

From the Firehouse to the Fireground

RICK LASKY   JOHN SALKA

Fire Engineering
BOOKS & VIDEOS

Copyright © 2013 by
Fire Engineering Books & Videos
110 S. Hartford Ave., Suite 200
Tulsa, Oklahoma 74120 USA

800.752.9764
+1.918.831.9421
info@fireengineeringbooks.com
www.FireEngineeringBooks.com

Marketing Manager: Amanda Alvarez
National Account Manager: Cindy J. Huse

Director: Mary McGee
Managing Editor: Marla Patterson
Production Manager: Sheila Brock
Production Editor: Tony Quinn
Cover Designer: Karla Pfeifer
Book Designer: Susan E. Ormston

Library of Congress Cataloging-in-Publication Data
Lasky, Rick.
  Five alarm leadership : from the firehouse to the fireground / Rick Lasky, John Salka.
    pages cm
  ISBN 978-1-59370-234-2
  eISBN 978-1-59370-833-7
1. Leadership. I. Salka, John. II. Title.
  HD57.7.L3747 2013
  658.4'092--dc23
                                        2012044568

Printed in the United States of America

6 7 8 9 10   16 17 18 19 20

There are so many people to thank and acknowledge, so many who have been there through the good times and the bad, so many who have mentored me, and so many who have helped me get to where I am in life today. *To everyone, thank you!*

My first family:

To the best friend I have ever had, my wife Jami. Thank you for always being there for me, supporting me, and helping me dream big. You are my "voice of reason" and work so hard for all of us. You're an incredible mommy, and to be honest I just don't know how you do it all.

To my son, Rick, a Fleet Marine Force Navy corpsman, thank you for being the best son a dad could ask for, but more importantly for what you have done and continue to do for our country. I am so very proud of you!

To my daughter, Emily, you are incredible! You are so driven, smart (just like your mommy!), and beautiful. Anything you do you are successful at, and I am so excited to see just where you go in the future.

To my dad, the very reason I am a firefighter. Thank you for introducing me to the fire service.

To my mom, the most caring person I have ever met. I miss you so very much!

To my sister, Doreene, *thank you!*

To my brother, Darren. You are and always will be in my heart. I miss you buddy!

My second family, the fire service:

You serve without prejudice, without fear for your own safety, and provide a model for others to follow when it comes to service. You don't do it for the money, and so many of you do it for free. You place the welfare of others in front of your own, and so often your first family pays a price for it. You define selflessness and thank God you still make house calls.

To those brothers and sisters who have given their lives for others: Thank you for your sacrifice. It was not made in vain and we are so much better because of all of you!

Never forgetting means never forgetting!

—Chief Rick Lasky

Writing a dedication for a book is never a simple task. There are so many people I'd like to recognize for their inspiration and support.

To my wife, Dawn, and my children: John, James, Maureen, Brian, and Colleen. They are the inspiration for everything I do. I thank them for being who they are and for helping me through my 30-plus year career in the fire service.

To the men and women of the FDNY who demonstrate every day that loyalty, passion, excellence, and service are alive and well in America. And to the officers and firemen of the 18th battalion where I worked my final years with the FDNY; all of the six companies are dramatically different from each other, yet amazingly similar in their dedication to the dangerous and dramatic work that we all do.

To my friends who make this journey more enjoyable and meaningful. Whether it was in a firehouse or on the road for a seminar or hunting in the woods, I am blessed to know you all.

To all of the firefighters everywhere who have answered their last alarm; doing the work we do sometimes ends tragically, suddenly, and without warning. The firefighters who didn't return from their last alarm were robbed of their futures and deserve our admiration and respect.

To Paddy Sullivan, a lieutenant with FDNY TL-58, who suddenly left us this year. Paddy was a fine officer, a dedicated firefighter, a respected colleague, and most importantly, a husband, dad, and a friend who will be missed by his family and his brothers on Tremont Avenue.

— Chief John Salka

CONTENTS

PREFACE

This book is a compilation of lessons learned, situations handled, decisions made, and problems solved. All of these issues, and many more, make up the core of the set of skills and abilities we call *leadership*. As we have said in leadership conferences and workshops all around the country, there is no defined set of leadership skills. Each of us has a unique blend of talents and specialties that we have developed over the years, and this book is no exception. The stories we will be telling, the problems we will be solving, and the teams we will be building in this book are ours. We have been firefighters, company officers, and chiefs in volunteer companies and career departments. We have both served in no fewer than three separate fire departments, and the stories in these pages are about events that occurred in the firehouse, on the training ground, at fire scenes—even off duty. The events we describe in this book may seem familiar to you. Lots of similar problems and solutions occur in fire departments across the country every day. We hope that the lessons we learned and describe in the following pages will be helpful to you in your specific situation.

As you go through the chapters and you find lessons, stories, or solutions you think may be helpful, feel free to underline or highlight the material. If you find other issues that you don't like or disagree with, cross them out. This is not a textbook but a learning tool. Like the tool compartments on your apparatus, the chapters are set up for you. Other departments might have a different way of arranging their tools, and that's just fine. This is not a "read once" kind of book. Keep it somewhere that you can refer to it when a difficult situation arises. It should be like a fellow officer who is always available for questions about difficult situations.

Read on and enjoy. As you develop new leadership skills, you will soon see the positive results they can produce. You will feel more like a leader and gain confidence in everything you do. Your crews will find that working with and for you is more rewarding and enjoyable, and they will be safer and more effective too. Your bosses will notice your increased and improved leadership abilities, and the people that we are all here to protect, the citizens in your communities, will be protected by a more professional, able, and effective team of firefighters.

ACKNOWLEDGMENTS

There are so many people who pass in and out of our lives, and all too often we forget to thank them for what they do for us. *Five Alarm Leadership* has been a labor of love for us for several years. Our lives, experiences, this book, none of it would have been possible if it were not for so many people. We would like to take this opportunity to thank just a few of those who have helped us in so many ways.

To the *Fire Engineering* magazine and FDIC staff: our brother and editor-in-chief Bobby Halton, Diane Feldman, and their incredible team, thank you for everything you have done for us over the years.

To PennWell Books: Mary McGee, Marla Patterson, Erich Roden, Brad Epperley, Cindy Huse, Mark Haugh, and a support team that is second to none!

Some of the best photographers in the country: Matty Daly, Rob Reardon, Tony Greco, Sheri Baldwin, Tim Phillips, and Gordon Nord. The phrase "a picture says a thousand words" would be an understatement when it comes to describing your work. Thank you!

To two of our nation's best fire departments, the FDNY and Lewisville (TX) Fire Department. Thank you for your dedication and service.

INTRODUCTION

The buggy slowed to a stop, and the chief stepped off into the cold New York City night. A bitter, damp December wind, soaked from the harbor surrounding the island, cut through his dirty gear like a knife. His knees ached, and his hands were sore from gripping trumpets, slapping backs, and helping to stow gear. His mind was still on the 11th Street job he just left, and he wondered if there couldn't be a smarter way to pick up gear, like the hose roller he built several years earlier. He wondered if there wasn't a way to save the men's backs when picking up after battling a fire. He was very aware of how many men were injured during salvage and pickup when the adrenaline was gone and the men's muscles, pushed to their limits during the fight, were struggling, weary and sore. He knew that that was a time when his men were extremely vulnerable to serious injuries, and many a sleepless night he spent trying to figure out a way to reduce those injuries. Tonight, he thought, would be no different, except maybe tonight he might have some solutions.

No sooner did his second boot hit the floor than the bells sounded. He turned for the man-door and his buggy. He thought for a second that he never felt as tired as he did right now, well maybe except when he served as a drummer boy for the 69th. Despite his being young and healthy, that was hard duty. Marching as drummer in the Civil War was the defining mark in his life's journey; he never thought the war would end. But he knew it would because the men he admired most in the world told him it would. The tenacity and perseverance he observed in those men, in his officers, and the senior men kept him and all the other younger soldiers going. Everything about those men was burned into his memory, but mostly it was their unfaltering commitment to duty that left an indelible mark on him. Their spirit and personality kept him going then and made him who he was today.

He admired those officers, the sergeants and old veterans: They never asked anyone to do something they would not do themselves. They never hesitated, they never complained. They pushed through; they inspired, innovated, and created an atmosphere in camp that convinced everyone that ol' Master Robert and his confederates were not invincible and that the union would prevail. He marveled at how they inspired him and those around him to fight the good fight, but that they never spoke poorly or ill of any of the Confederate soldiers. Rather, they often praised them and wished them well and prayed openly that this war would just end with no more death. They always had a piece of hard tack or some jerky to share with a hungry boy, usually their last bit of food. To a man, they always had a good word for all, and they made sense of the mission for a scared boy confused by the violent frightening world he found himself thrown into.

Now, more than 30 years later, as the chief of the Sixth Battalion, he was walking out to his buggy and toward his waiting engineer. A few seconds later, they were headed up to W. 23rd St. for a fire in a lamp factory. He knew the route by heart and, making the last turn, he sized up the street: He could see fire and strong smoke pushing out of the fourth and top floor, not a good omen. His men had pulled lines, grabbed a plug and their axes, and were making short work of the doors. Good men, strong backs, stout hearts, and skilled to near perfection in the use of their tools, his men, New York's bravest.

He gave his engineer a few requests to check and headed to the door, tightening his coat, setting his helmet, and looking over his crews. At the door, he mentioned to one burly Irishman that he was glad to see he had sobered up from his daughter's christening last week. The man continued to swing his ax and yelled, "Same to you, Chief," with a giant grin as the door gave out and fell inside.

The smoke had not hit the first yet, a good sign. He gave a wave to the two teams of hosemen lined up waiting behind him to follow; with assistant foreman John L. Rooney at his side, he moved quickly to the stairway. Assistant foreman Rooney was a winner of the Gordon Bennett medal for distinguished bravery for the rescue of a young girl who he coaxed into jumping into his arms as he stood atop a ladder, saving her from a fire. He trusted Rooney; the men trusted him, a good man, a good leader. Together, they led the way up three floors to the fire.

Directing the men to the seat of the fire, then stepping aside as they expertly applied the streams to good measure, he scanned the factory for extension. He examined the floor and stairs for integrity, and kept a steady eye above for collapse. He glanced at the streams dousing the flames and moving across the roof, breaking the stream into what looked like a heavy August rain drenching the fire. The fire had a strong head start, and the fuel load he knew was considerable, but with John Rooney by his side he had confidence that his men would hold this fire. Suddenly, the roof gave in without warning as the giant water tank's above weight was too much for the fire-weakened supports. The men worked as men possessed; they furiously struggled through their tears and frustration to free the chief Bresnan and assistant foreman Rooney, but it was too late. Both men died from suffocation under the crushing debris.

The story above is historical fiction. The facts are accurate and the legacy is documented. Many years ago, on December 29, 1894, a fire service leader, one who set a high bar, was lost in battle. Battalion Chief John J. Bresnan was an inventor, and among his many inventions were the Bresnan distributor, the hose roller, and a harness for the horses referred to as the swinging harness that was designed to facilitate faster response times in those days. It was said of Chief Bresnan that "no braver, abler, or more conscientious man then John J. Bresnan ever drew a paycheck in the service of the city of New York." It was noted that Chief Bresnan's entire career record was "unsullied" by any official complaint of any character. It was the obituary of a true fire service leader, of a true American.

The fire service in America and around the world for more than 2,000 years has been blessed with great leadership. The art and science of firefighting and its leadership require unique insight, deep passion, and tremendous humility. Every generation has found these humble giants in their mists. These giants understand that the art of leadership in the fire service is not about concepts; it is not about methods, traits, or styles—although they matter. It is primarily about character and empathy. The students of fire service leadership have marveled as we have listened to the stories of Leo Stapleton, Tom Brennan, John O'Hagan, Alan Brunacini, Andy Fredericks, Jim Page, Ray Orozco, Pete Ganci, and Emanuel Fried; we wonder how we would have measured up to the challenges they eclipsed.

As students of leadership, firefighters read everything we can on leadership and leaders; we study the greats and fallen, we relate to the words of wisdom from baseball players, Greek philosophers, military business leaders, and religious leaders. We marvel at how they faced adversity and challenge and, notwithstanding the outcome, how they lead others with honor and humility. Accomplishments such as that of Colonel Chamberlain, who was able convince his men they could hold the line on Little Round Top during the battle of Gettysburg as wave after wave of Confederate soldiers fell upon them. Then, when all seemed hopeless, his men, who were out of ammunition to fix bayonets, charged. They followed him, they trusted him; he had spent the time he needed to win their confidence. More importantly, he knew and cared for them, he respected their talents and their contributions, and they respected his.

As we learn from those who came before us, who lead successfully and unsuccessfully, we see how they did not really "get things done through others," as some leadership texts would suggest but rather they allowed those around them to use the talents they had to their fullest even those with whom they did not always agree. General Washington, for example, while during the miserable winter of the Valley Forge encampment, struggled to stop mass desertions, labored to rally a disloyal command staff, and wrestled in letter after letter to cajole support from a frightened and unresponsive legislature. Inspired, he turned to an enlisted soldier, a former editor, Thomas Paine. He asked Paine to compose something to inspire as he had done with his pamphlet "Common Sense."

Paine responded on December 23, 1776. While marching, he grabbed a drum and so his first American Crisis article was inked on the head skin of a drum.

He wrote:

> THESE are the times that try men's souls. The summer soldier and the sunshine patriot will, in this crisis, shrink from the service of their country; but he that stands by it now, deserves the love and thanks of man and woman. Tyranny, like hell, is not easily conquered; yet we have this consolation with us, that the harder the conflict, the more glorious the triumph. What we obtain too cheap, we esteem too lightly: it is dearness only that gives everything its value. Heaven knows how to put a proper price upon its goods; and it would be strange indeed if so celestial an article as FREEDOM should not be highly rated . . .

Washington had Paine's words printed and read to all; many feel it saved the revolution.

Throughout the ages, different men and women at different times have defined leadership in thousands of different ways. My friends who wrote the book you are about to read and enjoy would be embarrassed to be compared to Washington or Chamberlain, as they are humble men. The writers in the 1950s on leadership would have called them "Great Men," relating to the great men theory of leadership, which sought to define leadership by the traits a leader displayed—traits such as dependability, assertiveness, self-confidence, cleverness, persuasiveness, coolness under pressure—all of the traits Rick Lasky and John Salka have in abundance. In that regard, they are great men, but to a more important point, they hope to train, teach, and help all to reach the same level that makes them more than great; it makes them important.

As leadership researchers studied further through the years, it was decided that leadership was dependent on how someone acted, how they helped to generate activity among a workgroup of firefighters. It was thought that there were three basic styles: autocratic, democratic, and laissez-faire. They thought that a leader was either focused on work or focused on people, and that these three styles would be used to help get the job done on the fireground. Fire service writers back then thought that the situation created the style, that a fire officer on the fireground needed to be autocratic, but that same officer in the station could be democratic or laissez-faire. The general point was that different situations call for different kinds of leadership, different kinds of behavior. As you turn the pages of this book, you'll see that the authors will show you how they faced different kinds of situations and used different kinds of leadership styles, yet underpinning all of those styles were two important values: sympathy and integrity. Like Chamberlain, each of them has always cared deeply about everyone around them and because they always put honor above all else, firefighters have been willing to follow them even when doing so put them in grave danger.

Today we hear a lot about being a transformational leader, a leader who people believe inspires people to do better by igniting a passion within. Transformational leaders motivate firefighters by clearly and vividly providing a clear picture of a better way to do things, a more effective way to do things, or a fairer way to do things. The opposite of these transformational leaders are the transactional leaders, who use rewards such as money, praise, or recognition to motivate and, when those fail, use punishment or discipline. Rick and John are transformational; however, much like Thomas Paine, they understand that to be truly transformational, you have to be passionately committed. Like Washington, they recognize that to a much greater extent you must be intellectually honest and correctly aware of where that commitment to your vision will take those you are leading.

Genuine leaders like Rick and John take great pains to be absolutely aboveboard in everything they say and do, and that sometimes means using their position and authority to realign folks to our mission. And as you'll read in this book, Rick and John recognize that the true fire service leader understands the value of transactional leadership as well. The authors will show you several examples of when to use proper levels of discipline, not to hurt or punish but to provide direction to provide correction. To help realign individual behavior by making sense of the mission in a real world way so that every firefighter understands how their individual contribution is important, that the individual behavior reflects on us all and that we all depend on one another.

There is no doubt that Rick Lasky and John Salka are two of the most charismatic and extraordinary leaders in today's American fire service. They have made contributions to the fire service that have saved lives, improved our fireground effectiveness, and helped enhance the reputation of the fire service as a whole. They have dedicated themselves to the service of others and to something greater than themselves; and, in the course of their lives, they have proven their ability to lead. They have proven that they understand that their job is not to manipulate people but to create an environment in the firehouse, the fire station, and now the entire fire service that is conducive to continuous improvement and that adds to our traditional values and principles. They understand the difference between behavior and culture and work hard at trying to improve our normative behaviors, at the same time remaining respectful and dutiful to our culture.

On the pages that follow, you will see that John and Rick understand deeply the purpose of the American fire service, its value to the citizens, its importance in our communities, and its incredible place in the history of humankind as the placeholder of our greatest achievement—the ability to be willing to sacrifice oneself for another. That was the lesson that the old soldiers taught the young drummer boy: that there are things worth fighting for and things worth dying for. The role of the fire service leader is to make sense of the world and the mission of the fire service to the next generation. Rick and John do that on the pages that follow with incredible clarity; they share some of their most profound moments and some of their most important achievements.

In page after page of this incredible book, Rick and John quietly point out that a good firefighter has four qualities that are universal. These qualities you'll see in every story Rick and John tell; these qualities will come through as you listen to their words and envision their actions. Every quality firefighter is incredibly sympathetic or empathetic and has a tremendous ability to understand what another person is going through and how it is affecting them. They point out in story after story how important it is to have emotional intelligence, to have social intelligence, and to be kind to all. They point out that a good firefighter is a caring firefighter.

Rick and John provide us with the fundamental element of duty, that every quality firefighter is punctual. They understand how important it is to show up on time and to be there when they are needed and to be there even when you are not necessary, sometimes you just need to be there for others.

Being punctual shows that we understand duty. Being punctual shows that we respect others. Being punctual means you are courteous. It is small habits that matter most, and being punctual is fundamental to being a quality firefighter.

John and Rick deftly and subtly remind us that every quality firefighter has an unfaltering passion for training but, more importantly, an unrelenting compelling desire to practice. Training is learning a new skill, training is being exposed to a new methodology; practice is becoming a master of that skill or methodology. Practice is about the pursuit of excellence. Practice is the hallmark of a quality firefighter. Practice is not training. Practice is what Washington used at Valley Forge to create from a group of farmers and shopkeepers an army—not the strongest army but a proud army and a passionate army, an army that eventually helped establish the greatest country in the world—an army that understood its mission was to bring to life a nation devoted to individual freedom, a nation that will serve as a beacon to all who struggle to be free.

And finally, in this book, we get a look at the most important personal characteristic of a quality firefighter: humility. Rick and John remind us that a quality firefighter does not pound his chest. A quality firefighter is a quiet person; a quality firefighter thinks more of those they serve than they do of themselves. As you read this book, you will understand that John and Rick believe a humble leader is strong enough to take unpopular stances, that humble leaders lead by example, they tell the truth, they expect the best from others, they serve without complaint, they study hard, they enjoy hard work, and they always give the credit to others.

I was flattered and humbled to be asked to write this brief introduction. I would like to thank Rick and John for this incredible opportunity to have shared a few moments with you in this important book.

Respectfully your servant,
Bobby Halton
January 4, 2013

1
DEFINING LEADERSHIP

BACK TO BASICS

For decades the fire service has struggled in its attempts to strengthen the leadership traits of its members. Good, solid leadership programs have been few and far between. A catalog listing those programs would be pretty slim to say the least. There are many great programs developed by progressive fire chiefs and fire service leaders, but all too often many of them fall short when it comes to providing quality information to the officers and firefighters leading the way in the fire service. Where we, as trainers, often fall short is in providing real-life scenarios, situations, problems, and the proper solutions to handle those situations in the real world—not from some "canned" program but from real-life, everyday leadership challenges, the stuff that you can wrap your arms around that makes you a better leader.

"The strength of the group is the strength of the leaders."

—*Vince Lombardi*

Many papers and articles about leadership have been published, and they often contain good information, but where they miss the target is in providing our fire service leaders with the information and tools they need lead effectively.

Case in point: For years we've battled in our attempts to reduce line-of-duty deaths (LODDs) in the fire service. In the early 1990s, in our attempts to address the increasing number of LODDs, we developed two programs for the fire service that directly addressed training how to rescue a trapped firefighter or firefighters, or in some cases rescue themselves. The programs we developed were titled *Get Out Alive* and *Saving Our Own*. Both programs were dedicated to doing just that: getting your teammates or yourself out of a jam and saving firefighters' lives.

Shortly after developing and implementing these programs, we began to receive notifications of actual documented saves using the techniques taught in these classes. Firefighters and officers would call us and say, "What I learned in your class actually saved my buddy's life!" Considering that the average number of firefighters lost in the line of duty each year was 100, we began to believe that we were starting to make a difference, at least on the fireground. We hoped that the numbers would actually begin to decline. That's what we believed would be the result of these training programs.

Think about it: 100 firefighters killed in the line of duty each year. In the first year we taught these programs we heard about at least seven documented saves. The next year it was nine, and those were just the ones someone reached out to us to tell us about. Just think about how many we probably haven't heard about. We thought the number would decline from 100 to maybe 98 or 97, or even 95 LODDs. Yet even with all the training we were doing, year after year we saw the LODD numbers remain about the same.

We considered the possibility that one of the reasons the numbers weren't going down was that we were always adding firefighters as the fire service continued to grow. Unfortunately, this theory often proved unfounded since, in some parts of the country, fire departments were actually seeing a reduction in personnel. Others were closing firehouses and, in some cases, laying firefighters off. Some were just not hiring people to fill vacant or open positions, allowing them to evaporate due to attrition.

So again we began to examine the LODDs around the country, the reasons for those deaths, and whether those two programs were truly having an effect on firefighter survival rates.

The first realization was they were *indeed* saving firefighters' lives. No doubt about it. But why were the numbers not going down? As we looked at the fatalities and dug into the causes, we realized that we were weak in several areas.

One area in particular that really stood out was when a Mayday call went out. We were not managing those incidents properly. We were seeing more and more policies and procedures developed and implemented regarding the managing of a lost or trapped firefighter, but we weren't really training the incident commanders how to "manage the Mayday." We weren't training firefighters and officers in how to react to the Mayday, and at the same time we weren't teaching the trapped firefighters what they were supposed to be doing to help themselves.

Because of these shortcomings, we thought that if we developed a program that dealt specifically with managing the Mayday, we would be able to address that need.

With the help of Deputy Chief Skip Coleman, retired from the Toledo (OH) Fire Department, we were able to address that need through an article and training program we naturally titled "Managing the Mayday" (fig. 1–1).

Fig. 1–1. Toledo (OH) Deputy Chief (ret.) Skip Coleman

We were really proud of ourselves and thought that surely this would make the LODD numbers go down. Heck, the article even won a journalism award. Once again we were wrong.

Then one year, while the Fire Department Instructors Conference (FDIC) Advisory Board was gathered to plan and develop the next year's program and conference, we considered that maybe one area we weren't addressing in training our firefighters was in "the basics." Maybe if we addressed the basics of firefighting and emphasized that need in our training programs, we could cut down on the number of LODDs and injuries. Maybe we wouldn't have to jump out windows, slide down ladders, and tie ropes around firefighters and drag them out of buildings. Maybe if we got back to training our people how to "lead out" and stretch that initial attack line, or search a building, or handle those SCBA emergencies, maybe, just maybe it would move us in the right direction. Maybe through our training in the basics we could avoid those problems in the first place. We knew it was a big maybe, but what the heck? It was definitely worth a shot.

Maybe if we got back to training our people on how to "lead out" and stretch that initial attack line, search a building or how to handle those SCBA emergencies, maybe, just maybe it would move us in the right direction.

So we did, and that next year's FDIC theme was "Back to the Basics." An interesting point was made by one of the featured speakers at that conference. Retired Commissioner Leo Stapleton of the Boston Fire Department, while speaking during one of the morning general sessions in front of about 3,000 firefighters, made the following comments: "I noticed that the theme for this year's conference is 'Back to the Basics.' I have one question. Why did we leave them in the first place? We're not that good! Being proficient in the basics serves as the very foundation for everything else we do on the fireground. Granted, today's fire service is required to perform many tasks and train in many different areas, but when we fail to train in the basics, bad things start to happen." What an incredible statement from an incredible man, one of the heroes and legends in the fire service (fig. 1–2). So back to the basics it was. Unfortunately, the numbers still didn't go down.

Fig. 1–2. Boston Fire Commissioner (ret.) Leo Stapleton with Chief Rick Lasky

WHO'S FAILING WHOM?

What we noticed next in our travels across North America were some trends in situations that were popping up on a regular basis. Here's an example: We would arrive the day before we were to deliver a program or seminar, and often we were given the honor and privilege of meeting with the men and women of that fire department, or sometimes even several area fire departments. While visiting over coffee or during dinner, we would ask the question, "What's new? How are things going with the troops and the department? How's the budget?"

They would tell us that they just settled on their contract or got a new fire engine or opened a new firehouse. Most places had a lot of good things going on, but usually through those conversations they would bring up some of the not-so-good things that were happening.

One of the areas of concern that seemed to regularly pop up during those conversations was what fire chiefs were letting their firefighters do and not do. In several instances, the men and women we were visiting with would tell us that one of the big positives for that year was that they got to go shopping for the meal on duty again.

When we asked, "They don't let you go shopping for groceries while on duty?" their response was usually something like, "No, the chief feels that it's bad public relations." We'd then ask questions like, "How is that bad for PR? Do you go shopping naked? Are you doing something wrong while you're there? Do you park in the fire lane, which leads to setting a bad example? What's the big deal about going to the grocery store to shop for the meal while on duty? How did it get to that point? Did somebody do something wrong? Really, they won't let you go to the grocery store for what you need to make lunch or dinner? Really?" We actually did a public service announcement (PSA) on our cable station on why we go to the grocery store and that the city doesn't pay for firefighters' food and that they're available for calls, and citizens said, "Oh, that's not so bad after all."

If a fire department had that rule, then it probably had rules in place that you weren't allowed to turn the television on or watch it between the hours of 0700 and 1700. Firefighters might not be allowed to stand or sit in front of the firehouse in public view. We heard about all sorts of rules that didn't seem to make much sense.

The thing that is baffling about all this is that if we can't trust our fire-fighters to go to the grocery store and conduct themselves appropriately, if we can't trust our firefighters to stand or sit in front of the firehouse and act accordingly, if we can't even trust our firefighters to have the television set on during the day, then how can we trust them with a citizen's valuables or a half-million-dollar fire engine? How can we trust them to care for a citizen's baby in the event that that child needed medical attention?

We can trust them to make drug calculations in a nanosecond, but we can't trust them to go to the grocery store, sit in front of the firehouse, or to turn the television set on or off during the day? Doesn't that seem silly? To be honest, we would find it difficult to go to our staff chiefs and request them to take time away from hiring firefighters, protecting their budgets, building firehouses, creating safety initiatives, buying turnout gear and tools, and so on to write an SOP on what time to have the TV on or whether we can sit outside or go to the grocery store. What it really comes down to is that sometimes we get overly distracted by some of the simplest and silliest things going on and we forget to focus on the real issues at hand.

If things are not right in the firehouse, look at the company officer. What is he or she doing or not doing? It doesn't matter if the newest firefighter turned on the "wrong" TV channel or was acting inappropriately, it's still the company officer's job to set the attitude for the firehouse, to set that tempo, and to make sure that everything is going right with the crew and in that firehouse. When a weak officer allows improper behavior to go on or turns a blind eye, bad things happen and that bad attitude and environment carries right out of the firehouse and onto the fireground. Do you ever find it interesting that when you have a firehouse that always seems to be in turmoil or in trouble or is always filthy, that when the winds of change occur and the officer is moved to another assignment or firehouse, soon after the firehouse now assigned to that company officer becomes the one that is always having problems? *That's a lack of leadership in the firehouse.*

While these points were brought up by the men and women of the department the night before the program or seminar, the next night we would find ourselves catching a ride back to the hotel with the chief. That chief would usually bring up the topic of low morale and attitude issues within the department, and then ask for advice or suggestions about how to address those issues. One of the areas that we would often discuss was the fact that we get hung up on some of the tiny issues that really should be addressed at the company officer level, and in doing so we end up clogging up the whole system with minutiae. Ultimately that leads to a failure to communicate, and when that happens everything comes to a screeching halt.

Lots of chiefs have failed to keep those issues at a lower level and with the company officer. Instead they micromanage, and those little problems grow and fester into something big. Often the solution is just a matter of getting everybody together, talking and communicating, looking at the issues, checking the egos at the door, and making good, solid, commonsense decisions, without letting emotions get in the way.

Often, the solution is just a matter of getting everybody together, talking and communicating.

One example of this was evident when we were visiting with some firefighters in their firehouse the night before our program. We were enjoying a cup of coffee when we noticed some artwork on one of the walls. When we asked the crew what it was, they explained that one of their members had painted their station logo on the wall. And it was beautiful! A bald eagle in flight carrying an American flag in one talon, a set of forcible entry irons in the other, and a banner in its beak with a pretty cool saying. Nothing offensive, just a great statement of company pride. They very quickly said they'd really rather not talk about it and that it was kind of a hot button topic. Naturally we had to ask why, and they explained that when the fire chief saw the artwork on the wall he suspended the lieutenant for not asking for permission. Our response was, "He suspended the lieutenant for allowing his firefighters to paint *their* company logo on *their* wall?" There was nothing offensive about the artwork. Very quickly the reason for some of the other, smaller and in some cases silly, problems came to light.

The next day while we were presenting our program, we eventually got to the topic of company pride and how easy it can be to get that whole end of things going. One of the topics was that of company logos and their impact on a firehouse's attitude and performance (fig. 1–3). It may sound kind of simple and ineffective to some, but it does work. At the end of the day the fire chief came up to us and said, "Message received. What do I need to do to fix it?" Our suggestion was that on Monday, he should call in his union president and the suspended lieutenant, close the door, tell them you're not opening a formal labor management meeting or anything like that, and tear up the suspension order. Tell them that you really *did* think that the artwork looked great (that's what you said to us) but next time to "throw you a bone" and tell you so the next time one of your bosses (board member, councilman, etc.) says, "Hey that logo on the wall at station 1 looks great," you can acknowledge the fact that you actually know about it. Do what you can to reestablish, or maybe establish for the first time, a good line of communications. We told him that if that didn't work we would fly ourselves back out there at our own expense and take him and his family anywhere they wanted to go for dinner, our treat. On Monday at about one thirty in the afternoon, we received a phone call from the chief saying that he just had lunch with the lieutenant and his crew and that it had worked. As a result, this department became one of the leaders and examples of good labor-management relations and now serves as a model for others.

Fig. 1–3. Lewisville (TX) Firehouse #1 company logo. How hard is it to let the troops have a little company pride?

As a result of the information exchanged during these conversations with the firefighters, officers, and chiefs, a light bulb came on. One thing jumped out at us. It was a glaring indication of where we were really hurting ourselves when making sure everyone went home: *we were killing and hurting our fire-fighters before we ever left the firehouse!*

Before we ever left the firehouse to go on an emergency, before we ever turned a wheel, we were hurting and killing firefighters due to a lack of leadership in the firehouse. Before that firefighter got lost and disoriented and ran out of air, before that firefighter fell through the floor, before that firefighter had a building collapse on top of him, before any of the contributing factors to those LODDs occurred, we weren't doing our jobs back in the firehouse. We weren't training, supervising, managing, and leading our firefighters. We were failing our people *before* they ever put on their turnout gear. Sadly, we were failing to lead.

As we began to look at the leadership programs being offered, we quickly realized that we were missing our mark. Aside from a few good ones, many of the programs being offered were created for the private sector and for civilians. Even those that were developed for government employees were often dry and didn't address the unique demands of the fire service. It took an understanding of just how the fire service operated and the specific challenges facing firefighters and officers in order to create a tailor-made program specifically for leaders in the fire department. We wanted to build a program that dealt with the issues facing today's fire service, as well as the challenges going on right inside the firehouse. We needed to address *real leadership with real people*. By accomplishing this one task, we could begin to tie everything else together and to *really* make a difference in the lives of our firefighters.

SAME CIRCUS, DIFFERENT CLOWNS

This book is a project that happened by accident, but was also borne out of frustration. We started teaching a program—a very abbreviated version of this book—as an hour-long presentation called *Real Leadership with Real People*. It started out as something we were asked to do after some bellyaching about some issues at a meeting. That one-hour program grew into our presentation titled *Five Alarm Leadership*, and now we've turned that presentation into a book, so that the lessons we've learned in a combined 60-plus years of fire service experience can be passed on to future fire service leaders (fig. 1–4). We're very blessed, honored, and privileged to travel all over and meet folks while teaching, but what we *really* get to see when we're out and about is some of the nonsense that goes on out there.

Fig. 1–4. Five Alarm Leadership

During the program, we would often ask the students, "How many people know what happened at the tragic fire in Hackensack, New Jersey? How many people know what happened at the Waldbaum's Supermarket fire in New York City? Why do we have the codes that we do? Why do we do what we do?" And usually only two students would raise their hands. The point of this exercise was to make it clear that as leaders in the fire service we're not teaching all of the information that we should. A lot of the problems we were seeing were happening because of the poor leadership back in the firehouse.

We're here to talk about leadership. We're here to talk about how to deal with people, how to solve problems, how to make things happen, how to make the folks who work for you happy about coming to work and enjoy doing what they're doing. And we're also here to make sure they're doing their job well.

Leadership encompasses everything we do. You can't manage store fires without some leadership skills. You can't provide customer service without some leadership skills. You can't plan budgets without some leadership skills. Leadership affects everything, from tactical operations to public speaking. Your leadership skills, or lack thereof, are going to have a positive or negative impact on your ability to do anything. It doesn't just affect how you resolve conflicts in the firehouse, but how well your firehouse is run in general.

It doesn't just affect how you resolve conflicts in the firehouse, but how well your firehouse is run in general.

All the elements of what we do in the fire service are affected by your leadership skills. That's true whether you're a firefighter, a company officer, a chief officer, or a staff chief. Leadership skills are also important down at headquarters, whether you're a chief of training, chief of operations, or whatever level depending on the structure of your fire department. It doesn't matter where you are in the chain, whether you're the newest firefighter joining the department or if you retire next week after 35 years. Everybody's leadership skills affect the effectiveness of the company, bureau, county, or wherever it is you work.

We think you'll learn as you go through this book, through our positive *and* negative experiences, some lessons about what works *and* what doesn't work. By allowing us to explain some of the mistakes that we've both made, hopefully you can avoid the same pitfalls in your career.

EVERYBODY'S DIFFERENT

There could be 5,000 people in a lecture hall, and every single person's leadership skills and abilities are going to be different. You could even take two firefighters with the same career path—you and your buddy. You go to high school and college together, you join the fire department together, you work the same shift, you get promoted to lieutenant or captain or chief together, and as chiefs you're going to be dramatically different people. Even if you have all the same experiences, you're going to be different because *everybody* is different. Everybody's going to have a different angle on leadership.

We've picked up useful nuggets of information from the folks we work with, the folks we work for, and from the folks who work for us. We learned valuable lessons from firefighters when we were lieutenants and captains. We've received wise counsel from senior chiefs when we were coming up through the ranks, chiefs who took the time to mentor us a little bit. Of course we never used the word *mentor*; they just gave out some helpful advice now and then. I'm sure every firefighter reading this book has picked up some points, some interesting ideas, some concepts, and some skills about leadership from the folks they've worked with as well. Everybody takes something from someone. The question is, what do you want to take with you? What kind of a leader do you want to be? What do you want them to say about you when they're sitting around the kitchen table talking about the good leaders and bad leaders in your organization? Which column do you want to fall into?

What kind of a leader do you want to be?

That's the interesting part about leadership: it affects every aspect of the fire service. It's not just its own subject. Leadership is about everything, whether you drive a fire truck or U-Haul, whether you're a fire chief or a lifeguard. Leadership affects everything you do.

We'll also discuss some negative situations. Everyone has problems. Everyone has deficiencies. Everyone has some things that they don't do well. Everybody has some things that they could probably work on. We've been doing presentations in the fire service and private sector for a long time, but we still hand out evaluations at the end of our classes. These evaluations grade you on a scale from one to five. If someone circled a five, it feels good and all and it's fantastic that they think we're so great, but we don't really learn much from those evaluations. We look at the evaluations with a two or a three circled. Those tell us that somebody's not happy with something. *That's* where we have an opportunity for improvement. Everyone loves praise; everyone loves those pats on the back, but the only way any of us can improve is by focusing on areas where maybe we're not doing so well. Once in a while we need to stop reading and believing what's in our own news releases and take a good hard look at how well we're doing as a whole. Where do we need to improve? How well are we doing? Where are we missing our mark? With this kind of self-evaluation we can continually strive to be better at what we do, never settling for the mundane and "same old stuff" that no doubt leads to mediocrity.

> "Every now and then we all need to sharpen the saw."
>
> —*Gordon Graham*

THE COMMON DENOMINATOR

It doesn't really matter whether you're in a fire department such as New York City's that has 11,000 people and 210 engine companies, or the Lewisville Fire Department that has 150 members and six or seven engine companies, or even if you're in a small volunteer department.

The South Blooming Grove Volunteer Fire Department has one station. It has two engines, one truck, one rescue, and that's it. Their entire staff is about 35 people. That's about as small as you can get.

So what's the common denominator between New York City, Lewisville, and South Blooming Grove? People. Firefighters. Same circus, different clowns. Firefighters are firefighters. Anywhere you go—whether it's a big city firehouse, a small city firehouse, or a small rural volunteer fire company—there will always be one constant: the people.

On one hand, we can do a lot of things in Lewisville, Texas, with our little department of 150 people that they can't do in New York City. On the other hand, the FDNY can do a lot of things that the Lewisville Fire Department can't. In this book we try to address both sides of the fence, if you will. Whether you are in a big or small organization, you can never *not* lead.

Obviously there are some differences. Some big city firefighters work in the city and commute home 30 or 60 miles and don't actually live in the area where they work. Some features of that job are different from a small volunteer fire department where the firefighters live and work in the same town.

Whether you are in a big or small organization,
you can never not *lead.*

For all the little differences, when we talk about leadership, problems, conflicts, productivity, efficiency, safety, and all the other issues that are important to us, we find many of the most significant things are constant across the board. You put a helmet and a coat on, jump on a rig, and go to a fire. It really doesn't matter whether you're driving down state route 208 to go to a little house fire in South Blooming Grove or you're driving down Webster Avenue in the Bronx to go to a tenement fire, there are constants that we'll be able to talk about and share with you. We think you'll see that no matter where you are, it's always the same circus, different clowns.

WHY ARE YOU READING THIS?

We know we're preaching to the choir here. If you're reading this, you're taking time out of your life and money out of your pocket to improve your leadership skills. For some folks, reading this will be a confirmation. They will read everything we're talking about here and say, "Hey, I must be doing a pretty good job. I've got everything they talked about covered." Others may say, "Wow. You know, there are two or three things I could take back from this. I hope I never have that happen to me. I'm glad they went through that so I don't have to!" That's the whole point. We're here to help you sidestep some of the land mines that we stepped on during our careers *and* share some of our successes as well.

We hope there may even be some who will take this as a reawakening: "You know, I've been doing this for 25 years but I've been kind of going through the motions the past few years. After reading that I feel good about what I'm doing again. I remember why the fire service is the best profession in the world! I remember why I got into it in the first place."

I remember why the fire service is the best profession in the world! I remember why I got into it in the first place.

Whether you're a volunteer or paid firefighter or both, it doesn't matter. It takes a very special person to do this job, more so than any other profession on the face of the earth. I don't care if you're talking about doctors, pharmacists, teachers, or police officers. They all do a great job, but there's nobody, *nobody* like a firefighter when it comes to figuring out problems and taking care of people. It absolutely takes someone special to commit to this way of life.

Our best day is someone else's worst day (fig. 1–5). We don't want to see someone else's house burned up, but that's what we've trained for. Have you ever tried to explain what a good fire is to your neighbors?

Fig 1–5. Our best day is someone else's worst day.

Your next door neighbor asks, "How was your work day yesterday, was it busy?"

You answer, "Yeah, we had a good fire about two in the morning."

The neighbor always inevitably asks, "What do you mean by a good fire?"

It takes a special kind of person to do what we do. No normal person would go to his or her boss and say, "Boss, we need a job. We need a fire. I don't want to see anyone's house burn down, but if it's going to burn, let it burn on our shift so I get to go put it out."

That's the whole firefighter mentality. We don't want to see people hurting, but it's what we trained for. When they're at their worst, that's when we're at our best. Helping someone through all of that bad stuff, making the hurt stop or go away—all of it is an absolutely incredible feeling, one that is second to none. Helping people, there's nothing better!

When they're at their worst,
that's when we're at our best.

2

BROTHERHOOD

The same leadership skills are used effectively by church choir directors, managers at McDonald's, and the NASA engineers who ran the space shuttle program. Those same leadership skills are used in the fire service as well. Leadership is about dealing with people. It has nothing to do with what the current task may be or even with the job. It's about motivating people, steering them in the right direction, getting them fired up about their profession, and laying the foundation for success in your organization.

A good leader is a good leader is a good leader! That's why you see leaders jumping around from corporation to corporation. The CEO of some pharmaceutical company may be running NASA five years later. How can a single human do that? How can one person have the skill set required to lead in two such differing fields? Because the job isn't putting the pills in the bottle or putting the stock on the cart. The job is leadership. The job is putting it all together so that the people, the team, can get it done and feel the sensation of doing a good job; they can feel that something they just did made a difference, that what they do for a living matters.

Before September 11, 2001, the public always had a good impression of the fire service. People trusted firefighters. However, after September 11, people opened their eyes because they looked to the fire service and they watched how we operated through some very difficult situations.

After watching how we reacted to that tragedy, a lot of people in the general public said, "You know what? Firefighters must really have something special going with their operation."

A vice president and branch manager of Morgan Stanley, Alice Hughes, now retired, is a friend of ours. She said to us, "You guys are crazy. Your people go running into buildings when everybody else is running out. How do you get them to do it? How do you get your firefighters to follow you into a burning building? How do I get *my* employees to follow me into a burning building?" Here's an incredibly smart and powerful woman, a leader of a huge company, and she's asking us for leadership advice. But that's the kind of leader she is: always looking for that edge, that different way of doing things, those things that get you to the next level faster than the competition. It's the quest for information that makes you just that much better than the others. What started to happen after 9/11 was that people in the private sector started to realize that we in the fire service have something to offer in the way of a leadership model and how we operate. We're a family, an organization, a group of people, and a team like no other.

We went to a conference in San Diego to watch a very successful speaker, Marine Corps Captain Jason Frei (fig. 2–1). He's a fairly young guy, in his 30s, missing his right arm from the elbow down. He started talking about his experience in Iraq and how he was injured.

Fig. 2–1. Marine Corps Captain (ret.) Jason Frei

Jason told the story about him and his Marines going down the road one day in a convoy during the initial stages of Operation Iraqi Freedom, when there was an explosion. His driver turned to the side of the road, thinking maybe there was a problem with the transmission or that something in the motor blew up, because they were having trouble with the vehicles at that time. When he reached for the door he realized the door was bashed in and his arm was very badly damaged. Suddenly he realized it wasn't the vehicle that had blown up; they had been hit by a rocket-propelled grenade (RPG). A young 18-year-old kid grabs the captain and drags him out of the Hummer into a ditch.

They're stuck under heavy fire; everybody's shooting, and bombs are going off. Here's this young kid, sticking by his captain even in the middle of all that danger. Captain Frei said that the kid turned to him and said, "I've got my weapon and I've got yours. I'll get you out of here. Don't worry; I'm not going to leave you." The story went on and on. It ended with this 18-year-old kid carrying Captain Frei out of the mess.

Captain Frei has a unique perspective on the youth of America; he was saved by one. People call American kids lazy, uneducated, and unmotivated.

Not all of them!

Captain Frei said, "Here are these 18- or 19-year-old kids that were in the back of a car making out with their girlfriend and trying to graduate high school only a year before. Now this kid is telling me he's willing to stay there in a firefight and die before leaving me?" The question was why? The answer was because he's a Marine! Because he was taught about the brotherhood and loyalty and all that they stand for. Because of those things, he wasn't going to leave Captain Frei behind. He was going to stay with him.

"Experience is a hard teacher because she gives the test first, the lesson afterwards."

—*Vernon Law*

We should be able to produce that same effect in the fire service because we're very similar organizations. We can also both be the same thing to kids that don't have a big mission in life. Maybe they don't have a dream yet. Maybe they don't even have direction. Those kids can be influenced by good leaders. Captain Frei's story just goes to show you that it's not as hopeless a picture as people sometimes paint. When we look at kids today, we tend to focus on those few who are struggling instead of the millions who are doing some pretty special things. The future is bright, but it takes good leaders and mentors to pave the way for those that follow.

SUCCESSORS

One of the things we try to emphasize is succession planning: building tomorrow's leaders and successors. Building tomorrow's leaders is fine, but building tomorrow's successors is what's really important. There's a lot of paranoia out there about the next generation.

I should be the last outside fire chief they hire at Lewisville. That is if I'm doing my job. I told my boss, "We've got people prepared all the way up and down the line." Now I understand once in a while there are places where you get to the point when you've got to go outside for a fresh start. Obviously that's how I was hired, but when you've got a decent size department, it should be able to promote from within. It's sad that they feel they have to go outside because they have nobody they're comfortable with taking the reins and running the department.

I sit in on a lot of fire chief assessments for a couple of different search firms. We go interview the people making the decisions, and we constantly hear, "You know, we have a couple people from inside, but they're kind of weak."

I rarely hear one of the city managers come up and say, "Man, we've got John Salka. He's our deputy chief of operations, the guy's a home run;" or "We have one of our acting captains, Lisa Belanger, and she's dynamite!" (fig. 2–2); or, "I'm not playing favorites, but we've got a couple folks on the inside who are going to be hard to beat out. Somebody from the outside's going to have to come in here and really knock them out of the boat to take this job."

Instead I hear, "Well, we've got a couple of possibilities, but nobody we want to go with."

Unfortunately that's our own fault. We're not building tomorrow's leaders and successors. We're not building people who will reach and work toward the future.

Fig. 2–2. Acting Captain Lisa Belanger

"The more effort you put into hiring and promoting, the less time you'll spend fixing people problems."

—*Eric Harvey*

I see that all the time in our fire department. In New York City since 9/11, we've lost more than 4,000 people to retirement. Chiefs and company officers, mostly our senior people, retired, and we replaced them with young firefighters. My firefighters are very, very young. Every run I go on, I get out of the chief's car, walk down the block to the address, and there's a probie standing there. Often there will be two, sometimes even three of the four firefighters on the back step are probies.

With more than 11,000 firefighters and officers in the New York City Fire Department, there are probably not more than a few hundred firefighters who have been there for more than 20 years. Of course there are some officers who have been around for more than 20 years, but those are the more senior people. We have had a gigantic influx in the last few years of young people, which is actually very good. This is certainly a young person's job.

I'm 54 years old. You folks reading this may not be 50 yet, but I'm telling you it ain't easy, all right? I got the stuffing kicked out of me just about a month ago. I went to a six-alarm fire as the rescue battalion chief in the Bronx. I ended up on a fire floor where I encountered some of the most difficult and challenging conditions I have ever seen.

Earlier in my career I was a lieutenant in the squad, and I was a firefighter in a rescue company, so let's just say I've been to one or two fires in my time. Let me tell you, I got the crap kicked out of me six weeks ago! Two days later I was still smelling like smoke and still sleeping in the afternoon. It wasn't like the old days. I'm the old man, but this is a young person's job and I recognize that. Anybody else reading this who's a firefighter recognizes that as well.

That said, what's wrong with having a bunch of young people in a fire department?

Lack of experience.

Lack of knowledge, lack of tactics, lack of skills. Of course, they're not totally lacking. They get good training. We train them in the firehouse; they're on their way. Let's just say they're capable but they're not great.

The problem is that these young folks aren't sitting around the firehouse discussing all that they did right or wrong in the last fire. They don't sit around and tell each other, "Here's what you could have done . . ."

They're not doing that because they haven't had enough time yet to experience a lot of fires. We used to have senior firefighters sitting around the kitchen training young rookies. Two or three of the senior guys would jump in there and grab the young ones and say, "Come on outside, let me show you something."

Now it's not happening because most of our people don't have anything to show anybody else. They simply aren't experienced enough. They're all eager to learn, and we've got a couple of senior people around, but for the most part the officers have to do most of the training now. So we've got this gigantic young force in the fire department, and they have to get their experience somehow. Five years from now they're all going to have seven and eight years on the job, and things will be better, but in the meantime it's slow, even in New York City. Don't think every fire company in New York City, every engine and truck, is going to two and three fires a day. It's not true. Certainly plenty of them are, but there are plenty of places that are just doing a normal amount of work, a normal amount of running, and they've got to wait for experience to catch up.

A YOUNG PERSON'S GAME

Experience is the best teacher, I think we all agree. You can read a book like this, you can sit in a lecture hall, you can watch a video, and there are a lot of things you can do to gain knowledge, but actually getting out there and getting your hands on the tools, extinguishing fires, going to jobs, and stretching hoselines is the best way to learn. Unfortunately, it's also the most expensive and hazardous way of learning. What we recommend is a combination of learning in the firehouse, training and drills, and learning by experience as well.

When we sit around the firehouse, we look at some of these young firefighters with two, three, or four years on the job, and we can pick out the ones who are going to be sitting in the chief's car 10 or 15 years from now. When we're going down the Chattahoochee River or wherever we've retired to, some of these young firefighters, the lieutenants who are over in the front seat of these engines and trucks, are going to be the chiefs.

Now those of you who are the chiefs today, we certainly aren't kicking you out the door right now, but the bottom line is that this is your last stop. You make chief, you're on the way out the door. It's not the beginning of your career; you're on the downslide. The members at the beginning of their careers, the young firefighters and young officers, they are the successors. Those are the people who we want to break in and train so that when they get to the position that we're in right now, they are able to do a great job.

That's an important part of leadership, not just developing your own current leadership skills, but helping to develop the skills of your successors. Don't misunderstand, continuing education is very important, whether you're going to be a chief for another five years or only five more months. It's great that you develop new skills and that you're still eager to learn. More important, however, is that you young folks who are in your first four or five years in the fire department must prepare, because you are the future leaders of the fire department.

There's a young guy who works in a squad company in New York City. After September 11, when they suffered a loss, he would show up back to the firehouse and ask the senior firefighters, "Well, what'll we do? What'll we do?" And one of the senior firefighters would say, "Okay, come on, we'll go to the hospital and we're gonna check in." The more experienced officer took the lead and took the kid under his wing and said, "This is what we're going to do, and how we're going to handle it, and how we get through all this."

You must prepare, because you are the future leaders of the fire department.

A few years later, on "Black Sunday," they suffered another loss in the FDNY. The kid was actually at the call, and when he showed back up at the firehouse there were four or five young firefighters there asking, "What'll we do?" This kid took what he had learned and he said, "Well, first thing we'll do is we're gonna go to the hospital and check in, then . . ."

Do you realize what just happened? The changing of the guard. This kid had become the experienced "senior" firefighter without even realizing it. He was in that role that he'd always looked up to. These rookies were turning to him as he used to turn to someone else a few years ago.

That happened by itself. This firefighter had about five years on the job at the time. He got hired just months after 9/11, which is the demarcation point in our job right now. Everybody refers to everything in terms of whether it was before 9/11 or after 9/11. There are people who were not on the fire department on 9/11 who are almost senior people now. They have eight years in. They're almost considered senior firefighters. Obviously they don't have 15 or 20 years, but eight years under your belt is pretty good right about now. That senior firefighter we just talked about is a lieutenant now and still mentoring and grooming the next wave of successors.

CYCLES OF SENIORITY

The FDNY had a big hiring boom after 9/11. Some departments hired 20 new firefighters in one year, and for another 100 years that 20-year cycle is going to be in place. Each department has its cycle of seniority, how many people they have who are senior or not.

There are firefighters in New York City who have 5, 10, 15, or 18 years on the job who basically run the firehouse. Lieutenants can come and go, and captains can get assigned and then three years later get promoted to chief, and they're gone. There are some instances where a firehouse will have had five or six captains come and go, and the same firefighter is still there. That's the senior person who really sets the pace in the firehouse.

*That's the senior person who really
sets the pace in the firehouse.*

It's all about how leadership affects the successors and the people who are coming in at the bottom. We've talked a lot about how we should be teaching this. We teach "getting out alive." We teach "saving our own." We teach firefighters survival on the outside. We've been doing it for more than 20 years. We thought we'd be done by now, thought after 10, 20 years, it was waning. We were sure people would stop coming and the classes would sort of fade away, but they haven't, and do you know why? Because every year firefighters retire and every year we find someone new has joined the fire service, so every year there are brand new people to train. It will never end!

There is always a fresh group of people who don't know everything. They'll come to a leadership class or a tactical class or some other class to get trained to be better firefighters. This is a perpetual learning kind of field. You can't ever stop learning.

There are so many departments around that are booming now, and they're hiring nationally and they're promoting young members. This boom has nothing to do with 9/11 or the economy; it has to do with that cycle of seniority. That 20-year cycle goes by, and all of a sudden they're facing massive turnover. We see it all the time as we travel around the country, so this isn't just a big or a small department issue. It happens all over.

We've got people who come in to talk to us saying, "We're losing two-thirds of our seniority in the next five years. What are we going to do?"

That may seem like an emergency, but if you're in that situation you have to say to yourself, "All right, now we at least have some heads up." Now you can plan ahead and look into the future a little bit. A little later in this book we discuss some programs that both of us use to combat this situation.

If you recognize that cycle and see the end growing near, that gives you an opportunity to at least plan for it instead of being thrown into the "switch," when you wake up one day and all that experience and talent is gone (fig. 2–3 and fig. 2–4).

If you're aware of it, then you're a chief who can see that land mine ahead and plan for it. "Man, I'm losing seven senior people in the next five to ten years." In some places ten years is half a career. Ten years goes by like nothing, and if you aren't prepared for it you'll be complaining and yelling at all your young officers because they don't know what to do. However, if you didn't spend the time to train these young recruits and you knew it was coming, whose fault is it?

Fig. 2–3. Plan ahead to capture that knowledge and those experiences before your senior officers retire, because once they're gone, they're gone!

Fig. 2–4. Lewisville Captain Butch Flanagan performing his last inspection during his retirement ceremony after 34 years of service. A great leader, but when he walks out the door all that experience walks with him. Plan to grab as much of it as possible, before they walk out the door.

The final point we'd like to make on this particular subject is for those of you who are chiefs. We ask it all the time in our presentations: "Who's a chief?" Then we ask about whose lieutenants get any kind of training, whose company officers get any kind of instruction before or after they're promoted.

So often all that happens when someone gets promoted is that he or she is given a different color shirt or new collar pins, then sent off to another firehouse and told, "Now, you beep the horn. You used to sit in the back of the truck, but now you sit in the front seat!"

We know all the negatives there, and we're not here to tell you how to run your business, but if your department doesn't do it already, consider sending your people to a conference to attend a leadership class for company officers. It's worth its weight in gold.

If it were possible, you could have every lieutenant come into your office and sit down with you for three hours just to talk about your whole career and all the lessons you learned. That would be ideal. Unfortunately no fire chief has the time to do that. Other options are to send them to a conference or a training program or hire somebody to come in and run a class. If finances are an issue, get together with the other departments in your district or your county and run a training session for company officers. They need the training and the tools that come with it.

The point in these types of exercises is to cut down on bad experiences. Everyone has had negative experiences. Everyone learns during their time on the job, their time at fires, and their time dealing with people. However, not everyone has to go through all the negative experiences we did. That's why we wrote this book about the experiences we've had, both the positive and negative ones, so that readers can be successful and avoid the pitfalls. Learning those lessons yourself can be a costly experience. We've been through it; we know. So in order that your young people don't have to learn those lesson themselves, let them learn from somebody else's mistakes.

THE ONES WHO REALLY NEED IT

At the end of most of our presentations, you know what we hear most? "The people who need to be here aren't here." And everybody knows the people we're talking about. You've probably got one in mind right now.

We were in Atlantic City with Hanover County (VA) Division Chief Eddie Buchanan, another great leader and role model, and he asked us, "When do you think we're going to see more good fire chiefs coming up? When will we see more of the good than the ones we get frustrated with?"

The answer was, "Well, in about 35 years."

"Thirty-five years?"

Unfortunately, sometimes things take a while. As long as we have commissioners and mayors and city managers hiring fire chiefs, for the most part they're going to say, "This is who we want." Oftentimes the people with the most knowledge on the subject, actual firefighters, are ignored in the job search process.

You may think to yourself, "How we can affect those decisions? We don't even get any input." The answer is that the more quality that we can get out there, the more that we can increase the pool with the "good ones." The firefighters who care about the job, the officers who care about their firefighters, the people who really want to make a difference—those are the types of motivated people we want in leadership roles in the fire department. If you don't get to take part in the decisions about chiefs in your community, then you need to start doing what you can to increase the size of the pool of that talented group. When that happens, some of the other ones who are just kind of hanging out will naturally be reduced.

The firefighters who care about the job,
the officers who care about their firefighters,
the people who really want to make a difference—
those are the types of motivated people we want
in leadership roles in the fire department.

Good leaders aren't born, they're made. You have to get your younger firefighters the training they need so that they can grow into good leaders. You ask them to attend conferences. You hold training seminars. You provide them the tools they need to grow into quality people who can lead and train the future members of your department.

You can tell the difference between the firefighters who really want to be there in order to make a difference and the ones who are just going through the motions. You don't give up on anyone, but you can get to the point where you say to yourself, "I'm wasting time with this person right now. I'm going to keep at it, but I've got a lot of good folks I'm neglecting because I'm spending time with him. I'm going to move that person to station 12, the 'land of the clay people,' and prop him up there. Here's his cup of coffee and a crossword puzzle. He can just sit there for a shift." You'll come back the next day and there he'll be, still sitting with a cup of coffee and a crossword puzzle. The tools will still be rusted, the rig still won't start, the place will still be a mess, and that person will still be complaining about not getting paid enough. We're not wasting any more time on that one. We're going to go have some fun with the movers and shakers who are going to make a difference.

Unfortunately there are a lot of people like our "land of the clay people" firefighter in the fire service, and they're hard to convert. However, some of their bosses won't even try. One boss we know would come out of his office and scream, "If this was the private sector, I'd fire half of these people!" Then he would walk back into his office and say, "I don't understand why these guys just don't appreciate the job, you know?" His folks aren't doing what he wants, so he makes the situation worse by terrorizing them, saying nasty things.

What we're trying to say here is that good leaders will inspire more good leaders, but even the best leader sometimes needs help. If you have some really promising people coming up, but you don't have enough time to spend with all of them, send them to a conference, bring a speaker in to talk to your department. Whatever investment you put into those young folks, we can promise you it will come back to your department tenfold.

3

MANAGERS ENFORCE RULES, LEADERS PROMOTE VALUES

MANAGERS OR SUPERVISORS?

Anybody know the difference between a manager and a supervisor? You're at a dinner party and someone says, "I'd like to introduce you to my husband. He's a manager at Quick Trail Company."

What does he manage? Do you know what managers do?

Managers do things right and leaders do the right thing.

Managers do things right
and leaders do the right thing.

Does a manager deal with people? Sometimes, maybe. Lots of managers deal with people, but some never have to. There's a manager at a truck stop right now working all alone. Maybe this manager hasn't talked to another employee all day, just showed up and turned on the lights, yet is called the manager of operations. Managers don't necessarily deal with people on a regular basis.

Supervisors, by definition, are supervising other people. A supervisor deals with people more closely than a manager.

You can't just be a great leader and expect everything to happen. There are other skills you need to have to do certain jobs, but leadership skills are the most important if you want to move up in the fire service. There are all sorts of titles in both the private and public sector: supervisor, manager, director and company officer, shift commander, district chief, and all the other titles that we have in our particular fields. No matter your title, it's the leadership element that is the *most* important. It's the leadership element that really has a defined impact on your mission, whatever that mission may be.

> "In order to move in a positive direction you have to lead in a positive direction."
>
> —*Rick Lasky*

It doesn't really matter what the mission is—it could be putting baked bread into a plastic sleeve properly before loading it on a truck—good leadership will define how well that job gets done on a consistent basis. Now, we know our mission is a lot more important, a lot more intricate, and a lot more dangerous than putting bread on a shelf in a store or serving beer in a bar, but the point is the leadership element of being a manager or being a supervisor affects everything. It's a defining element of whatever the undertaking may be.

People come up to John all the time and say, "I loved your management book!" (fig. 3–1).

His answer is, "Thanks, but it's not a management book; it has nothing to do with management. It's about leadership."

People don't really know the difference between the two; they just blend both topics into one. They think leadership and management are synonyms. Of course we want leadership and management to go hand in hand, but leadership and management are different.

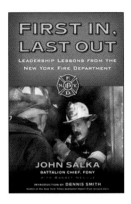

Fig. 3–1. *First In, Last Out: Leadership Lessons from the New York Fire Department* by John J. Salka Jr.

We have people all the time come up to us and say, "Can you tell me the difference between a manager and a leader?"

The difference is *managers enforce rules* and *leaders promote values.* Managers do it right; leaders do what's right. In today's fire service, do you have to be both a manager and a leader? Absolutely! Both skills are necessary, but we really believe that in order to be successful in the fire service, that scale has got to be tipped just a little bit toward the leadership side.

We'll be the first to tell you there's a business side to what we do. We never used to believe it when we were firefighters sitting at the kitchen table in the firehouse, but now that we have to deal with budgets and politicians and contractors and all the rest of the less-than-exciting stuff, we've realized that there's definitely a business side to the fire service. You can be a manager at a business just making sure people come in and sign for their paychecks and never really get involved and manage what you've got. Don't get me wrong, that's important and necessary, but the definition of a good leader is kind of like the definition of a good communicator. A good communicator is someone who tells you to go to hell in such a way that you look forward to the trip!

The definition of a good leader is someone who can get you to do things as a team, to meet the goal, sometimes without you even knowing it. They don't have to take all the credit. It's almost sneaky the way a good leader can somehow get you to do things without you knowing it. To be honest, good leaders don't want or need the credit. They know where it should go: to the troops, those who make it all happen.

"A good leader takes a little more
than his share of the blame, a little
less than his share of the credit."

—*Arnold Glasow*

Do you know a company officer or a chief officer who's not such a great manager but who is a great leader? The job gets done, no matter what. Even though these types of leaders may struggle a little bit with some of the technical aspects of execution, their leadership skills overwhelm the problem. That type of person will be one of the most successful officers around. Compare that example to another officer who has great management skills. That person may have been a CEO somewhere, but lacks leadership skills. These types of people can have tons of diplomas on their walls, trophies on their mantles, and thousands of other amazing accomplishments that wouldn't amount to a hill of beans at the firehouse, because nobody there follows trophies; we follow leaders.

These types of people can have tons of diplomas on their walls, trophies on their mantles, and thousands of other amazing accomplishments that wouldn't amount to a hill of beans at the firehouse, because nobody there follows trophies; we follow leaders.

★★★★★★★★

PARENTING

Leadership is like parenting: nobody does it the same. Each person's method is at least a little different because each person's experiences are different.

No two people in the country have the exact same fire experience, the exact same leadership experience, the exact same educational experience, or the exact same family experience. Every person in your building, in your city, and all over the country is unique. Because of that fact, everybody's skills and abilities are going to be unique.

I have five kids at home, which works out really well for me because I also have five kids at the firehouse. Leadership starts with your parents. The first leaders in my life were my parents. They taught me a lot of skills as well as some tough lessons. The thing is, you can't tell by looking what kind of parents someone has or what kind of person he or she is going to be.

When my wife and I moved upstate, about 60 miles north of New York City, we did our best to blend in with the community. My wife was born and raised in Manhattan and I grew up in Long Island, so we were a very long way from any place we'd ever been. This was a big move for us.

One night while we were out, we met another couple. When we came home I remember saying to my wife, "Boy, those two we met tonight were weird company. Let's hope they don't have any kids!"

Of course my wife scolded me and told me to be more sensitive, but I'm just not a sensitive guy. From my perspective, these people were just a little off. Well, guess what? They did have kids. One of them is now a cop and the other one is a schoolteacher.

These parents had somehow produced two intelligent kids who were making positive contributions to society. I would never have predicted that.

I also know a guy in the fire department who is as straight-laced as they come. Every seven days he gets a haircut. Every six and half days in the summer he cuts his grass to exactly five inches. His car is polished up the first Thursday of every month. This is a guy who is very structured and neat. Everything in his life is in order. This is the type of person you would expect could raise kids to become productive members of society.

One of his kids is in jail; the other has a purple Mohawk and a tongue ring. That's something else I would never have predicted. From all outer appearances, this guy looks like he's straight out of TV. His kids should be perfect. Yet his kids are screw-ups and the other not-so-normal couple managed to raise two of the better citizens in that town. It just goes to show you that you can't judge parents by how they look. The same goes for the firehouse. You can't tell just by looking whether a fire officer is a good leader.

Everyone does it differently. There are lots of ways to be a good parent, just like there are lots of good ways to be an effective leader. That's why you always need to learn from other people. Hopefully you're going to find some useful methods as you read through this book. Some of what you'll read here may be absolutely useless to you, but others might think it's the most important thing they've read in the whole book. We're going to provide a lot of stories and ideas in these pages; it's up to you to decide if they can be valuable to you in your career.

Successful leaders and successful parents have one thing in common: They have several different methods of getting things accomplished. When your kid is crying, sometimes you have to try 10 things before you find something that works. Any parents reading this know what we're talking about. It's the same way with effective leaders. They'll keep trying different methods of motivation until they find one that works. You can't just find one method and stick with it, though, because you're likely to run into a different crew somewhere along the line, and your standard methods won't work on them. Good leaders will adapt to any situation.

Another common thread between good parents and good leaders is their core values. At their root, their foundation, good leaders have a strong set of values. If you have a good set of values at your core, then whatever you do and wherever you go, you can be successful.

*At their root, their foundation, good leaders
have a strong set of values.*

NASA

Nothing happens without a good leader. Take the National Aeronautics and Space Administration, or NASA. It's a great organization. When we teach classes in southern Florida, we meet a lot of people who work there. This organization has had its fair share of trials and tragedies. The most recent one they faced was when the space shuttle *Columbia* broke up during reentry, causing the loss of seven astronauts. Before that, the *Challenger* exploded with teacher Christa McAuliffe and six others on board. Even back in the early years with *Apollo 1*, astronauts Grissom, White, and Chaffee all died during training in a fire on the launch pad. If you're old enough to remember that, you know what a huge tragedy that was. It can be devastating to an organization when something goes wrong on that scale, when lives are lost.

How does an organization like NASA stay in business? How do they get past that? How do they come back after such a monumental setback like that? Good leadership.

Just because you make a mistake, just because you have a bad day, just because you have a tragedy, that doesn't mean you don't have high quality leadership. There are some great firehouses that have had firefighters killed in the line of duty. There are some great companies that have people get badly injured in fires, but because of their leadership skills they are able to pull themselves up and keep going after such setbacks.

It's when things are going bad that having quality leadership becomes even more important. When people get killed, whether it's at NASA or a much smaller organization, good leaders are needed to help with the recovery. Both NASA and the fire service have some of the best leaders in the world. Most organizations wouldn't be able to recover after a tragedy on the level of the *Challenger* and *Columbia* disasters. Probably no other organization in the world could recover after going through what we lost on 9/11. It's a good thing the fire service isn't like any other organization in the world!

When something goes wrong at NASA, its leaders don't throw their hands in the air and give up. They figure out what went wrong and do it better the next time. They learn from their mistakes and get better. We're doing the same thing. The FDNY has pulled itself back up by its own bootstraps and become a stronger organization after that tragedy. You have probably experienced an apparatus accident or something of that nature in your firehouse that was a low point. What did your leadership do? If they're good leaders, they figured out what the problem was and took steps to keep it from happening again, thereby improving the entire department for the future. When things go bad in Lewisville, the first comment you'll hear from our leadership is, "We're better than this!" We've trained, we work extremely hard at what we do, so we expect more. Then you'll hear the question, "What did we learn?" Without looking at the whole picture, evaluating it, and looking for that constant move or means to improve what we do, we are bound to see the same failures time and time again.

We were doing a private sector teaching gig at Opryland in Nashville, and a lot of the folks there worked for Boeing, Lockheed Martin, and NASA. We had a chance to sit down and visit with a woman who was instrumental in running the space shuttle program. We asked her how she got through the *Challenger* disaster. Were there any special tools or techniques she used to get through it? She said that they had to continue because their mission is about more than just the astronauts and flight engineers. It's about the future.

The catalyst for them, she said, was that they have some tremendous leaders. These are people who don't lose their minds after a tragedy. They get together and say, "Okay, we had a setback. Now what do we have to do in order to keep this thing going?"

Take a look at sports teams. We've all seen a team that had a roster full of great players who continued to struggle for some reason. They have plenty of great players but they aren't winning. What are they doing wrong? When that same team picks up a new coach, two years later you see them in the championship. What changed? The leadership. *That's* the value of effective leadership (fig. 3–2). It can take a losing team and turn it into a champion.

That's the value of effective leadership. It can take a losing team and turn it into a champion.

And it's not just sports. Something as average as building a house or serving as a scout leader requires strong leadership. If you go to a construction site you won't see someone there with stripes or wearing a lieutenant's hat, but you know someone is there running the show. Someone is there beating the drums and making sure everyone shows up on time and does the right job. It doesn't matter what job you're involved in, the leadership skills are what will get you through.

Fig. 3–2. A good coach can make all the difference. New York Giants Head Coach Tom Coughlin and Quarterback Eli Manning

A WORKING OFFICER

The success of an organization depends to a great degree on its leader's ability to supervise, inspire, and train.

Most of the people reading this will either be getting ready to promote or have recently been promoted. We know how difficult it is when you're promoted to go from being someone's buddy to being his or her boss. Many people have major problems with that transition. Being able to supervise properly can make that shift much easier to deal with.

You can't be the firehouse clown one day then turn around the next day and expect that people will respect you just because you changed shirts. It has to start early. If you want to be a leader, you have to start early in your career (fig. 3–3). You're not going to supervise people if you're not willing to step up and make that commitment from the very start.

Fig. 3–3. Dallas (TX) Battalion Chief Stu Grant operating at an incident where a plane crashed into a house. Chief Grant began preparing early in his career to lead, and the payoff has resulted in him being one of the most respected chiefs with Dallas Fire Rescue.

There are two kinds of officers. I've talked in many classes about my buddy Eddie Enright, known by his friends as EE. Eddie retired from the Chicago Fire Department after 38 years as deputy district chief. He's an incredible man. It was an honor just to teach with Eddie.

He's an imposing six-foot-four Irishman, cool as a cucumber at an incident (fig. 3–4). People could be jumping out of windows, and he'd just lean over casually and say, "Hey Rick, we got some jumpers." Nothing shook the guy.

Fig. 3–4. Chicago Deputy District Chief (ret.) Eddie Enright

One time I went to a firehouse with Eddie. It was a single engine house, a fairly busy place, and when we walked in there was no one around. We found the firefighters in the back of the firehouse just sitting around, one of them wearing another fire department's t-shirt. The station was filthy, the rig was filthy, the tools were rusted, and we didn't see the lieutenant anywhere. So we sat down and started talking to the firefighters. Finally the officer came downstairs, and he was wearing a white t-shirt and white socks, which I know drives Eddie nuts. At this point Eddie went back out to the buggy (old term for fire chief's car), came back in with a sheet of paper titled "The Chicago Firefighter," sat down with the lieutenant, and started to talk about uniforms and honor and tradition.

An entire hour I sat there listening to Eddie talk about duty, honor, pride, and tradition. About how important our uniform is and what it stands for. That day I stole a "golden nugget" of wisdom from Eddie. He told this lieutenant, "If you were killing bugs for Orkin, if you were the Orkin bug man, you'd have to wear a uniform. Why can't you wear ours, be proud of what it stands for, and respect it?"

After Eddie had finished lecturing the lieutenant, we got back in the buggy and headed to another firehouse. This one was in a very busy district. A lot of action. When we got there the lieutenant assigned to the tower ladder came walking over. I couldn't make this up if I tried. The lieutenant was wearing a white t-shirt and white socks. I pulled up a chair and said to myself, "This is going to be great! I know what's coming now!"

I listened as they talked about the drill for the day, a fire that was in another battalion, some personnel issues, and a fairly long list of other things, but nothing about the uniform—nothing! An hour later we were leaving, and I said, "Please don't move the buggy. What just happened there? We just spent an hour with the lieutenant in the other firehouse talking about uniforms, but this fella does the exact same thing and he gets nothing. No duty, pride, honor, tradition, uniform stuff, nothing. I was expecting you to tear into him."

Eddie's response was, "Joe's a working officer."

I said to myself, "That's it? Joe's a working officer?" Then I asked, "What do you mean he's a working officer?"

He said, "The other guy had a lucky Saturday and lucked out on promotion day."

I said, "Eddie, you've got to explain this to me."

Eddie looked at me and said, "The other guy I can never find. You saw some of that. Not only can I not find him in the firehouse, but I can't find him on the fireground. Everything you saw in the firehouse—the dirty tools, the dirty rig, the messy kitchen, nobody wearing the proper uniform—that's how they work on the fireground. If someone doesn't take care of the firehouse, their tools, or the rig, then they won't take care of their job when they're out there."

Then he started talking about the second guy. He said, "Joe, on the other hand, gets in there early, checks out his troops, does his own size-up, has coffee, does his paperwork on time, and spends time with his people. He's not afraid to go out and roll a length of hose with the troops. He won't do the whole job for them, but he's out there with his firefighters helping them throw hose. He doesn't hide in the watch office pretending to be working. He'll walk out on the floor once in a while and say, 'Break time. Come on, I just put on a fresh pot of coffee.' Then he'll get them to sit down and talk about their day, the fire on the other shift, their kids, etcetera. When we went into Joe's firehouse, did you notice something? When Joe walked over, all his people walked with him. When he sat down they all sat down. They're like little ducks. Everywhere he goes, they go. In the firehouse *and* on the fireground as well. It's not that they're afraid of him because he's their boss. They just want to be around him. He inspires them to be better firefighters."

Eddie continued, "I could go to Joe and say, 'Hey, how's Tommy doing with his degree?' Some officers might just say, 'He's good,' but Joe really knows his troops. He'd say, 'He's doing okay, a lot of work for him but he's working hard at it all. We set part of the day aside to help him study, but right now my biggest problem is dealing with Johnny. He's got a sick kid at home and it's really bugging him.' Joe knows his folks and he knows what's going on. He knows the names of their spouses and their children. He takes an interest in their lives (both in *and* out of the firehouse), and they know it. *That's* a working officer, so I cut him some leeway."

There's the difference. We talk about inspiration and supervision, and that's a perfect definition right there in Joe. Eddie told me, "You know what? As much as it drives me insane—the white socks showing with your black shoes—in Joe's case I can turn the other way because I've got a list three or four pages long of people who are dying to work for Joe. I've also got a list a page and a half long of good firefighters who are dying to get away from the other guy."

That's the big difference between a working officer and someone who isn't when it comes to leadership.

4
SUPERVISION

Supervision is a word with a bit of a negative connotation. What does supervise mean, exactly? When it comes down to it, supervisors just make sure stuff gets done. When bad stuff is happening and things are going wrong, someone's going to have to deal with the problems. We've dealt with this ourselves. We were firefighters. We were company officers, lieutenants, captains—now we're up to chiefs. As we rose through the ranks, we both started to have more and more responsibility placed on our heads. That comes with the territory. If you don't want to deal with more responsibility, then you probably aren't ready for that leadership role.

If you don't want to deal with more responsibility,
then you probably aren't ready for that leadership role.

Sometimes being a supervisor isn't the most comfortable thing to do. Anyone who has been in a supervisory position has, at one point or another, had to "apply some supervision" to an employee. As a company officer, have you ever had to apply some supervision to someone you worked with? It's not the most fun thing in the world. Nobody wants to be the bad guy, but it's necessary. Without supervision, the rig doesn't get checked all of the time; without supervision, some may find it easy to do things that a good supervisor would never let them do. The kind of stuff that gets you in trouble or at times hurt.

"Being responsible sometimes means pissing people off."

—*General Colin Powell*

One thing we can promise you is that you're not the only person to notice that something needs to be done. The silent majority knows who's performing and who's dragging. Many of them have even probably thought, "I wish somebody would say something to those people. They never pull their own weight around here." Everybody in the firehouse knows that person who never stays a minute late, never gets there a minute early, doesn't care about the firehouse, the rig, or their tools, and seems to be just hanging out waiting for payday. If you're the person in charge, you're obliged to do something about it. As a regular firefighter, dealing with issues like that wouldn't be part of your job. But once you are promoted to a position of leadership, that is the very definition of your job. And more often than not, the troops are waiting to see what you're going to do about it.

We've both had to do it. We never enjoy it, but we've done it a hundred times. It comes with the territory, with that level of responsibility. If either one of us has a firefighter who we think may be going by the wayside, when it's "our turn," we'll sit him or her down and have a little discussion. It may be rough at the time, it may get a little loud, but by the time a week had gone by, that problem would be on its way to being solved, and in most cases, the relationship with that firefighter would have been strengthened. Once we got it straightened out and the person knew what was expected, we got on the same channel; it worked out for the best.

It's just one little conversation. We could have chosen not to have that conversation, because it isn't enjoyable and it would be easier not to bother; however, if we don't have that conversation then we aren't doing our jobs. Simply put, people want to be led!

Simply put, people want to be led!

THAT'S NOT FAIR!

Let's go back for a moment and touch on what was mentioned earlier about those two officers, the "working officer" and the one who "had a lucky Saturday." Does that seem fair? Two officers in same battalion, working for the same chief, both of them wearing white socks. One gets lectured for an hour and the other one gets a friendly conversation over a cup of coffee. Is that a problem? Is that supervisory discretion or inequitable application of the rules?

Some books we've read on management will say that is a problem, but we don't think so. That's one of the great benefits to being a good officer or being a good leader: You get to add a layer of flexibility in some situations if it means we're getting more out of it in a positive way than if we took the stance of living in a black-and-white, written-in-stone world.

For example, let's take some probies and young kids. They have to follow every rule, every time. As they get more time under their belts, things will lighten up on them a little. You can't be as strict on your veterans as you are on the rookies or you'll chase them away. On the other hand, if you let young kids form bad habits early, they'll never break them.

Sometimes you need to apply rules a little differently for different people; a good leader can sort that out. Any really good leaders you've seen will have the ability to read people and recognize what type of inspiration they need. Do they need a gentle reminder, or do you need to lean on them? As a good leader, you'll be able to tell which method to use in each situation.

> "The test of leadership: Turn around and see if anyone is following you."
>
> —*John Maxwell*

We had a company picnic in the middle of the summer back when I was the captain of Engine 48. The whole company was there. There were captains and lieutenants and all the firefighters from both companies in the firehouse. It got to be two o'clock, three o'clock, three-thirty, quarter of four, and the guys from my firehouse were saying, "Well, who's working tonight?" There were just a few of us who were at the picnic who had to leave and go to work the evening shift. I was the lucky captain who had to work that night.

A few of them said, "Oh yeah, I'm working tonight, too," so at that point I knew who was going to be working with me later. We all agreed that we should be leaving the picnic soon to get to the firehouse on time for the night tour. Soon after that, I left and headed to the Bronx.

I got to the firehouse, showered, changed, sat down in my office, and now the shift change rolls past and one guy hasn't arrived. Where is he? He was at the picnic. He even told me earlier in the day, "I'm working tonight with you Cap, I'll see you later." Yet there I was, sitting on the night shift and he wasn't at the firehouse.

He comes in ten minutes later, sneaks past the officers, doesn't stop in and say, "I'm really sorry I'm late." Instead, he runs upstairs and tries to get away with it. I finally ended up having to go look for the guy. I asked a couple of firefighters, "Hey, where's Bryan?"

Ten minutes later, he comes down to the office all spruced up and sits down and says, "Hey Cap, what's up?"

I said, "Hey, what are you doing?"

He said, "What?"

I responded, "I saw you three hours ago at the picnic. We all talked about getting here to work the night shift and everybody else made it, but you're late."

Now, I know that some people might think I was a bit strict. Coming in ten minutes late isn't a big deal. I've come in ten minutes late plenty of times. My problem wasn't that he came in late; the problem was what he did after he came in late!

What do you do when you come in ten minutes late? Everybody reading this book has been late for work at least once. Think back to a time that you arrived at the firehouse late for some reason or another. What did you do when you walked in the front door?

First off, you probably didn't walk, you ran! If you were smart, you ran to the company officer and said, "Hey boss, I am really sorry."

It's not this guy being late that bothered me; it's how he dealt with being late. He came in ten minutes late and I was sitting right there in the office. I heard the door close; I looked up and saw somebody go by; it was him. Instead of stopping in and apologizing, he was trying to sneak in so he could stay out of trouble. Instead of avoiding trouble, he just dug that hole a little bit deeper.

BLACK AND WHITE

First off, let us say that we're not telling you to go out and break all the rules. Rules are there for a reason. They increase our safety and raise the likelihood that we make it home at the end of the shift safe and sound, and with all of our pieces and parts. That said, if you live in a world of black and white, you're going to have an extremely difficult time. When you see things as only black and white, you cut yourself off from a lot of innovative and creative solutions.

Sometimes you have to see the world in black and white. Let's take the Internet for example. We've got Internet access at our firehouses. A while back the city purchased a software program that monitored your browser history. All the officers received special instructions on advising their personnel where they could go on the Internet and what sites they could visit. Not that anyone was doing anything wrong—it was a preventative measure installed to keep anyone from straying. It wasn't anything too bad, but we still had to sit down with some of the troops and tell them, "Hey, you can't visit or spend time on certain sites."

That was pretty clear cut. Then came the topic of emails and accessing personal emails on city computers. City regulations say that we "cannot use city equipment for personal use." When one of the firefighters read that and asked "Can we use the city computers and Internet to view personal email?" our city ITS director answered by saying that is was one of those 'gray' areas, kind of like the city phone system. They don't want to forbid the use of the phones for personal calls, but are also trying to be realistic and understanding with the employees. So, the understanding on the city's part is that we use common sense and not abuse the opportunity and keep the calls under ten minutes. That's the same stance on the personal email issue. Bottom line: don't abuse it, and always remember that what you view on the city computer system is all "open records"—viewable to the public and never private—so it goes back to the common sense thing. We are always in the "fish bowl," so use good judgment and stay professional.

With that type of minor issue, it's just a judgment call on your part as a leader. While it's not a big deal to let folks check email, often it's best and only a minor inconvenience to ask them to check it at home. Today with smart phones it's a little less of a problem. On the other hand, sometimes you'll see departments that won't allow firefighters to wear personal cell phones or pagers while they're at work. They're so worried about "double dipping" or "distractions" that they've made their firefighters miserable with strict interpretations of the rules, kind of like telling your teenager not to send a text message.

Here's another example of how we need to insert that whole common sense thing again. This very issue popped up in Lewisville when we received a call from one of the assistant city managers regarding a complaint from a citizen pertaining to a firefighter/paramedic answering a personal cell phone call while caring for a patient. The firefighter in question was kneeling over the patient when his phone rang. He didn't answer it. Then it rang again and he did, saying, "I'm with a patient right now, let me call you back." The patient heard the caller say "this will only take a minute and . . ." and then the firefighter hung up. Then the phone fell out of his shirt pocket and onto the patient. Not good! This brought about the "If you can't control the issue of personal cell phone use, then we'll order that they be left off from the moment you punch the clock at the start of your shift until you punch out." That message was given to the shift captains. End result: they did their job. The message was delivered by the officers and we haven't had an issue since and that was years ago.

We've all had to deal with that strict interpretation issue many times. Once there was a training exercise being put on outside of town at the local airport. This airport was literally two minutes outside the city limits. We had planned to send a company there to take the training course, then they'd report back to the rest of us on what they'd learned. Now understand that they are not out of service, just on delayed response. The remaining companies in town would have to pick up their slack as they do when we handle other assignments.

As we're planning this exercise there's a knock at the door. It's the union president. He says, "Boss do ya have a minute? I'm afraid we've run into an issue. I just got a call from one of the guys and he told me that we were going to be going to train outside the city at the airport."

I said, "Yea, it's a great class and a great opportunity."

He says, "But you can't do that. It says in the contract that anytime you send a company out of the city on a call or for training you have to hire a replacement crew back at time-and-a-half. I understand that you want the troops to go out and train at the airport, but the guidelines in the contract state that we can't take them out there without hiring back."

So my reply was, "So that's how it is? You're going to hold me to something that was negotiated twenty-five years ago when we were the only paid department around? We're going to live in a world of black and white. No compromises? Okay. Turn back in that contract where it says that 'The chief shall approve all leave.' The next time one of your guys comes in on a Saturday and sees that there are extra people and wants to take the day off, find me! Call me, page me, I'll get back to you later that day."

He replied by saying, "Hold on boss, the captains do a great job handling that now, we don't need to do that."

And I said, "But it's in the contract, right there in black and white." Then I said "flip forward a few pages where it says that you can't use city equipment or property for personal use." Effective immediately, personnel will no longer be able to wash and perform light maintenance on their personal vehicles; use the city computers for personal email or personal use; complete any 'home projects,' or use the city telephone system for personal use. We'll forbid the use of personal cell phones and pagers, and we'll put pay phones back in the firehouses. The only phone that will dial out of the city system will be the company officer's, who will be required to keep a log of those 'official business' phone calls. Then we'll make sure that everyone is in uniform at the start of shift. "You see there are only three of us who have to live by that contract on this side of the wall. You have three shifts full of folks that will all have to. We'll be writing people up right and left for not following the rules, and what's in the contract if we're going to live in the world of black and white." I said, "Do you know what this means?"

And he said, "I guess we're going to be going to the airport for training today."

Fortunately, this was a great union president with a great reputation both in the firehouse and out. We got along great and we could always talk things out; we made for a good labor/management team. He realized, as I did, that we needed each other. We knew that there were going to be times where we needed to compromise and work with each other. The rules are the rules, and contract are contracts—no arguing that—but common sense has to play a role once in a while, and we will always find ourselves in a position where we need to communicate and work through issues, together. That makes for good leadership on both sides of the table.

The point we're trying to get across here is that some rules should never be broken, like entering the fireground in full turnout gear and SCBA. Other rules, like training outside the city limits, can be bent on occasion without causing major problems for firefighters or their leadership. The two Cs (communication and compromise) can take you a long way as a leader.

The two Cs (communication and compromise) can take you a long way as a leader.

I'm not embarrassed to say this: Two nights before leaving Coeur d'Alene, Idaho for the Lewisville job, my good friend and mentor Alan Brunacini, asked me if I was sure that I wanted to move from Idaho to Texas. He said, "Texas is a great state with great people and all, but are you sure you want to leave here?" He reminded me that I was given this great gift in Coeur d'Alene with great people, a great union, great bosses, and everything else up and down the line, and that sometimes you only get one opportunity at that. He said he just didn't want me to go there and a year later be saying, "What did I do to my life?" Well, honestly he scared the crap of me.

Before I started the job, my wife and I were going to take two weeks and vacation on the way down there. Bruno scared me so much that we drove almost straight through. I couldn't wait to get there, but when we arrived, I realized soon after that we had a whole lot of problems; worse than guys who were just breaking rules—we had some really serious issues.

I'll tell you, I was pretty distraught when I first started down there. I was downright depressed. I knew we had some really good people, but boy did we have some issues to sort through.

That's when I was blessed to have dinner with both Bruno and another mentor, Tom Brennan, while at FDIC West in Sacramento (fig. 4–1). They asked me what was wrong, and I told them I've got big issues going on: I've got a couple of guys who might get fired, a couple more who might get suspended, a bunch of write-ups, and a whole lot of counseling to do.

First off, Tom says, "Whoa, whoa. Slow down a second. Take a breath and realize that they are a product of their leadership environment. No one has either shown them what to do or how to do it, or defined what was expected of them, and most of all, held them accountable if they had. They're just doing what they think they're supposed to, and yes, in some cases, that's leading to some bad things. When there's a lack of leadership in an organization or firehouse, that's what happens, kid. Maybe you should give them a 'do-over.' Push the reset button and tell them it's starts over, right now. Most will get it and catch on."

Fig. 4–1. Chief Tom Brennan and Chief Alan Brunacini at FDIC West, when I needed them and their advice most!

Bruno then asks me, "Have you had a chance to instill your value system yet?" I said, "No, I've only been here a little while." Then he said, "You've got to give it a chance to work. You can't just go in there chopping down trees and torching the place without giving them a chance. Is there a pride in the environment? If they have pride in what they do and not the best leadership skills, then that's an easy fix. You have to push the 'do-over button' Tom's talking about and you can't just expect them to get this stuff overnight. You've got to give these guys time to adapt to your system. Instill a system of values and give it some time. You'll see. Things will change. They always do."

Thank God for their advice. Some of the guys in the middle of some of that stuff are now some of my best captains and chief officers. These were perfectly capable leaders, but no one had ever held them accountable before. They were allowed to get away with so much for so long that they got used to it, and that lead to others doing things that they shouldn't. You know how they say that sometimes you don't realize you were given a gift until way too late. That was probably the best thing that happened to our department. It changed us on so many fronts, and all for the better. We're a better place because of it, and chock full of great leaders and people.

I've sat through a couple of grievance processes where someone was upset because we didn't hold everybody to the same rules. Someone will come in with a single example and say, "You didn't treat so-and-so that way." It's true, we didn't treat that person that way, because it was a first mistake. The person filing the grievance makes them all the time. That's why he or she got dinged this time. There has to be a process of progression when counseling or disciplining someone, and prior offenses and the seriousness of the offense have to play a role if you, as the leader, are going to make the right decision. What it really comes down to is common sense, and a system of objectivity and fairness. You just have to use common sense and be fair when you deal with your team—they'll respect you for it.

Now don't get me wrong, you can't just allow people to break the rules. Let's take John's firefighter after the picnic showing up late. The rule is broken, he's late. What I do about it depends on a lot of things: It depends on exactly what rule was broken, in this case being late. It depends on what the history is. Is this guy chronically tardy, or was this a one-time thing? Also the way you go about it can be different. Some people need to be leaned on to get a reaction and others just need a quick word in the office.

If you treat your troops fairly, then they'll like working for you. Try to inspire them with your behavior. Be a role model for the firefighters underneath you, because I can assure you they're watching. From the new firefighter to the company officer, everybody under your command is watching how you carry yourself.

You set the standard of behavior for the people underneath you. If you're a slob who's always late, then guess what kind of firefighters you're going to get? On the flip side, if you take care of yourself and work hard, then your people will look good and work hard, too.

TRAIN ON EVERY RUN!

You have to lead by example. If you want to inspire, then be inspirational. Be excited about your job! It's the best job in the world! It shouldn't be too hard for you to get pumped up about fighting fires. People will see how you act and they'll follow your example.

That same idea needs to trickle down to everyday training as well: You can't just turn it on for the big fires, but slack off in training. Professional football coaches would say, "You play how you practice." You can't skip training. That's our football practice. If you skip training, then you won't be ready for the game.

Training is very important. No matter what or where, you should have an organized training program, maybe your department has a training officer—most places these days do—but all should be using the company officer for training as well. This person has the best opportunity to train the team considering call volume, assignments, etc.

If it's the company officer who jumps on that rig every time you go out, then you can use every run as an opportunity to train. If you see somebody perpetuating bad habits on a run, don't hold back. You should always be on the lookout for opportunities to make your team better.

For example, you can use an automatic fire alarm to train firefighters to think about other situations (fig. 4–2). On a fire alarm call, you'll probably have people all over the building. Firefighters will be on their rigs, on the roof, and on the floor where the activation was reported. Another team will be standing around waiting to stretch hose if they're alerted that there's a fire.

Fig. 4–2. Take every opportunity to train your firefighters. Chief Salka with FDNY Lt. Tim Klett, an excellent company officer, discussing tactics after an incident in the Bronx.

If you're just hanging out while they're doing their investigation, go up to a control person—the firefighter responsible for measuring the hose—and ask some questions. Ask where the alarm was reported, what floor. This will be vital information if a hoseline needs to be stretched. The control person should know right off the bat that the alarm is on the fourth floor. Second, you might ask how many lengths would come off if a stretch needed to be started right away. Again, that's vital information a lot of firefighters don't think about until they're actually stretching hose. If the control person already knows the answer, you may shave a little bit of time off the operation which could, in turn, save lives. Is it a deep building or a shallow building? Would it be a four-flight stretch? These are questions you can ask to sharpen up your troops. Every run is an opportunity to drill. Training isn't just for prescribed training hours. Train all the time.

When you come back in from a fire and everybody's just sitting around the table eating sandwiches, take that as an opportunity to train. Ask your team about the last run (fig. 4–3). "Did anybody notice the hatchback on that car? Both of the cylinders had exploded before we got there." It doesn't have to be a big official training drill for you to teach your people lessons. There are dozens of opportunities for training every day. If you really pay attention, you could find five or six opportunities to train your members every shift. Everybody has room for improvement. It's your job to find those opportunities to teach your team so that they can become better firefighters and better people.

Fig. 4–3. Take time when at the kitchen table to discuss the last run.

ANYONE CAN LEAD, BUT NOT EVERYONE IS A LEADER

You don't have to be a company officer to be an effective leader. Some people who aren't leaders in the firehouse take what they've learned into the community, where they become very effective leaders. One may run a local scouting troop. Another is the president of the PTA. There are two town supervisors in New York who are retired from the FDNY. Firefighters are full of energy and possess tremendous leadership skills. Even if they chose not to be company officers and lead in the firehouse, they may use what they've learned there in other areas.

A lot of people are happy just being firefighters. They don't necessarily want to move up the ranks in the fire department, and that's fine. Thank God there are people who are happy to be firefighters! They do all the hard physical work. Those are the ones who get the job done, and it's nice knowing that there are people out there who just love doing the job.

We're not saying chiefs aren't really working, but the average firefighters out there getting their hands dirty are the ones doing the hard work. They want to stay on the job with an axe in one hand and a Halligan in the other. They may not be leaders in the firehouse, but when you get to know them, you'll learn that they lead in other areas of their lives. Leadership spills over from the job into everything else.

We've also all dealt with poor leaders. Just because it reads "manager" on the door, that doesn't make the person behind it good at leading people. We've all known a leader—let's use the term boss—who just shows up, but never shows any actual leadership. Sometimes you see this when a fire officer is at the end of his or her career.

This boss will walk into the firehouse, past all the troops who are just hanging out, straight back to the office and close the door. Some will barely say, "Good morning," before disappearing for several hours. Some may have another job they're working on in there; others may just go in there and sleep. Whatever they do, they're not showing any kind of leadership for the younger firefighters in their houses.

What happens when a firehouse is saddled with a poor leader? We find that someone else usually steps up. If the person who is supposed to be leading a team isn't doing their job, there's usually a natural leader in the group who will. Some senior firefighter will step in and say, "Okay everyone, let's go. I'm not a lieutenant, but we've got work to do today so let's get started."

The FDNY has institutionalized that leadership role among senior firefighters. They take care of a lot of business in the firehouse. Some firehouses have senior members taking care of the company account or "house tax." In New York City, just about every fire company has a house tax account. That's a bank account for the company, whether it's a single engine company with twenty-five firefighters, or one with multiple rigs and twice that many members; they all have one. All the firefighters pay $10 or $15 per pay period, so it ends up being a nice chunk of change. Some houses leave that account in the hands of the company officer, but others don't let the company officer near it. They have a senior firefighter who collects the dues, reminds anyone if they're late in paying, and cuts the checks. That is the person who will go out and buy a new flat screen TV for the firehouse or a new air conditioner if one breaks down, so it's a very big responsibility and an important leadership role within the company. The point is, there are opportunities for leadership everywhere. You don't have to be a lieutenant before you can be a leader.

THE PROBIE

In the fire department, it's not always the officers who make the rules. When a firefighter gets promoted to lieutenant, that usually involves getting moved to a new firehouse. When that same lieutenant makes captain five years later, another move occurs. You won't stay at the same place if you're a lieutenant or captain; however, a lot of firefighters stay in the same house for a long time. Those are the people who really set policy. They don't do anything without the consent of the company officer, but those long-term folks are usually the ones who really set the rules around the firehouse.

When the probies get out of school, after sixteen weeks or so, they are assigned to a company. The movie *Ladder 49* did a good job portraying that experience. What company you go to as a probie is a very big deal. The probies gather up their coats, their boots, all their gear and head to their new firehouses. In New York, they still have brass rails around a lot of the firehouses and a watch enclosure out in front. There is always a firefighter there, 24 hours a day. Every three hours a new firefighter takes a shift. They answer the phones, receive the alarms, and even answer the door.

When the probies show up for their first day of work and knock on the door, the first person they're going to see is a firefighter. Some of the other troops will gather around and start grilling the new members. They want to know how probie school went, where they finished in their class, how old they are, and if they play a particular sport. You know, all the important things. They'll talk about family and outside jobs, just the general "getting-to-know-you" type of stuff.

Then they'll send the probies up to see the boss. They'll get a lot of the same questions about family life and training, then they'll get the formal introduction. "Shift starts at nine a.m. Six o'clock is the beginning of the night shift. You might want to get here a little early. Here's your locker. Here's your schedule. Welcome to the team." Once all the basic information has been passed on, the lieutenant cuts the probies loose. They're not in the firehouse an hour yet and really don't know squat. Now comes the real education when they go back downstairs (fig. 4–4). That's when the leaders in the firehouse will pull them aside and inform them about all the important rules and expectations they should know.

Fig. 4–4. It's everybody's job to train the new guy. Senior firefighters need to share information and their experiences with the new firefighter.

"You talk to the lieutenant? Good. Now we're going to tell you how we do things around here." It's nothing really contrary to what the officer said, but now they give them the really important stuff. "Here's what we do at this firehouse. We start at nine o'clock in the morning here but normally everybody comes in at eight. That means you'll be here at seven thirty because you've got to be the first one in, right? We get cut at six o'clock at night or at nine the next morning if you're working twenty-fours. When somebody comes in at five o'clock in the afternoon and says, 'Who in the engine wants to go home?' It isn't you. You're the last one to go home, right?"

"Now, if you come into work and the bulletin board in the kitchen says, 'Tommy Reilly's mom passed away. Wake Monday and Tuesday, funeral Wednesday,' you need to know that if you weren't scheduled to work Monday, Tuesday, or Wednesday, well you are now. Somebody here wants to go to Tommy Reilly's mom's wake and/or funeral, so covering for that person is part of your job. If a member of the firehouse gets a medal, you'll be at the ceremony. If we're having lunch to celebrate it, you're one of the lucky people who have to set all that up. You can also plan on getting home two hours after it's over because you'll have to help clean up afterwards, too."

On and on the rules go. We all know them because we've all been there—the unwritten rules of the firehouse. They'll tell them what's expected of them, not by the captain or the lieutenant, but by their fellow firefighters. It's all part of the break-in period. None of those people are paid to do that. They aren't technically in any supervisory roles. There's no manual they can point to. That kind of informal leadership that everybody does, taking a trainee under your wing, can make the biggest difference.

That type of mentoring should continue all the time. After a run, older firefighters will pull the probies aside and give them pointers. They can teach them tactical lessons, the proper way to carry tools, the whole rundown because they know what's going on. The point is, leadership is everybody's job. It's not just the boss who can be a leader in the firehouse. Everyone can help coach the new probies along.

PART OF THE TEAM

We were giving a presentation one time and, during the break, a firefighter came up to us. He said, "I need to talk to you. You just mentioned how you deal with probies, how all the firefighters in your company help out and everything else. We got some new people at my firehouse, actually they've been there for a couple of years. They're good guys. They never miss a shift, but they never come in early, either. They work hard at fires, but in between if something happens they're never there. If somebody's mom or dad dies, they never come to the funeral. When someone in the firehouse is moving, we all show up to help but these guys don't. They don't come to stuff off-duty. I'm just wondering what to do?"

We asked him, "How long have you been there?"

He said, "Oh, I've got ten years on the job."

"Then the answer is simple: it's your fault."

He said, "What? How is it my fault?"

We told him, "If those people have been there for a year or two, and they're not doing the right thing, apparently you didn't tell them. You have to clue them in. You didn't tell them what was expected of them. And then you didn't, of course, follow up." Firefighters have no problem following up on other firefighters. Sometimes bosses have a hard time supervising people, but firefighters never have a problem supervising junior firefighters. They won't shy away from asking, "Hey, where were you yesterday? We were all down at the lake. You weren't working, and you weren't at the lake. Strike one."

We just threw an under-performer out of one of our firehouses not too long ago. Well, let's say he "transferred out." On paper, it looks like he transferred, but he didn't transfer. We threw him out. He was on the engine. The engine's captain came up and said, "Look, this guy's got to go. He's had three or four chances. He doesn't do this, he doesn't do this, and he doesn't do this. The guys are tired of him and we want him to go." So, we basically threw this guy out of the firehouse. Why? Because he wasn't playing ball. He wasn't part of the team—he wasn't doing what's expected of him.

We told the firefighter at the seminar that day, "If your probies aren't falling in line, if they're not contributing, then it's your fault for not telling them what was expected of them." It's not just the captain's job, or the lieutenant's job. It's not just the officially designated boss who has to do the training. Oftentimes it falls on that person, but the average firefighter has just as much responsibility to lead in his firehouse as the captain.

5

THINK OF A GREAT LEADER

When we think of great leaders, several individuals come to mind. Such legends from the fire service as Leo Stapleton, Tom Brennan, and Alan Brunacini would be at the top of that list. There are also great leaders throughout history we can look to as examples. Over the years, we've come up with a list of some of the greatest leaders in history. Your list may have some other people on it, either good leaders from your personal life or other historical figures you look up to. The following are some of the people we respect. Feel free to use some of the people from this list for your own. Everyone is different, so everyone's list will be a little bit different, but that's not important. You could have six or eight people just from your job on the list. This is just our small list, but we hope you'll understand why we've discussed them here.

DWIGHT EISENHOWER

Let's take Dwight D. Eisenhower, for example. Do you know what it was about Eisenhower that made him such a great leader? Obviously, he was the president of the United States. We all know he was a high-ranking general. The question is, what did he do before that? How did he make his way to the highest office in the land? Was he a private in the military who fought his way up the ranks? Was he a regular enlisted man? What battles did he fight? What path did he take to end up leading the greatest army, and ultimately the greatest country in the world?

The answer is that he was an administrative officer. Sure, he worked his way up the ladder, but he did it from behind a desk or at the side of one of his bosses as an aide. There are officers in the fire department that do it that way. Officers in the police department manage to go all the way to the top positions that way, as well. They may not get out in the field a lot, but they work hard at training centers and at headquarters. We're not knocking it, but most of us would rather be on the line than sitting at HQ behind a desk all day. Thank God there are people out there who are willing to do those jobs, though. They allow the rest of us to do our jobs. Without the people who do those administrative jobs, fire departments across the country would collapse.

The point is, Eisenhower didn't have a big, ribbon-filled career. As a matter of fact, during World War I, many of his peers had distinguished themselves, but Eisenhower never left the United States—a fact that very much disappointed him. Instead, his time was spent training troops who others would lead into battle.

Hard work, loyalty, being that "good soldier" with a proven track record helped to pave the way. It wasn't long before Eisenhower earned George Marshall's trust, and that Marshall saw him as a man who had the vision to execute the strategy the Allies had agreed upon. When he got to the top, how did he do? He did really well. The guy had tremendous leadership skills that he developed on his way up the ladder. At West Point, "Ike," as he was referred to, was described as the kind of person who had the knack of saying the right thing to gain others' cooperation. He had a strong personality and his overwhelming good nature inspired trust. His classmates regarded him as a natural leader who looked for ways to smooth over disputes and organize a group's efforts toward a common goal. Under the stress and strain of World War II, he performed flawlessly due to years of preparation and practice.

> "Great leaders are almost always great simplifiers, who can cut through argument, debate, and doubt to offer a solution everybody can understand."
>
> —*General Colin Powell*

Another major advantage that Eisenhower had, a skill shared by all great leaders, was his ability to team build and delegate (fig. 5–1). Great military and political leaders have the ability to surround themselves with high-quality individuals. When the time comes to delegate tasks, they can be confident when handing them off because they've surrounded themselves with people who can get the job done.

Who did the majority of the work in World War II? Omar Bradley and George S. Patton. These were two guys who couldn't be more different in their leadership styles. They chose vastly different paths to arrive at their moments of leadership. When the time came, Eisenhower needed both of them to step up.

Patton had an incredible ability to get things done, and Ike knew it. Most people have seen the movie, some of which is true and some isn't. One thing that is true is that Patton was a taskmaster. On the flip side of the coin was Omar Bradley. Eisenhower has said that he needed Bradley to be the "soldier's general." Eisenhower was very sharp in the way he used his people. Here's a guy who hadn't held any major commands or won any big battles before becoming a general. He didn't have the experience himself, but he knew how to pick his team. He was a master at surrounding himself with good people who could get the job done.

Fig. 5–1. Generals Clarence Huebner, Omar Bradley, and Dwight D. Eisenhower decorate the troops of the U.S. 1st Division.

*He was a master at surrounding himself
with good people who could get the job done.*

There is a story about General Douglas MacArthur and Dwight Eisenhower: Eisenhower had worked for MacArthur as a clerk early on in his career. After Eisenhower had completed his military career and was running for president, MacArthur was asked what he thought about his former employee. MacArthur replied, "He'll make a fine president—he was the best damn clerk I ever had."

That is Eisenhower's military history. He was an amazing clerk. He was an extremely intelligent man and a guy who could get things done, whether it was in an office or on a field of battle. He may have come from humble beginnings, but he rose to the occasion in a big way when he was called upon. He used leadership skills and shrewd delegation to accomplish his goals. People like that do not only enjoy successes, but learn from their failures, too. That's another quality you'll see in good leaders.

MORE MEAGER BEGINNINGS

Another great American leader experienced his fair share of failure in his life. Sometimes it's people's failures that mold them into great leaders. Leaders who have never known failure might not know how to handle the situation when it finally strikes. People who have suffered that loss before not only know how to handle it better, but develop more of a drive to avoid it. Once you've tasted failure, you're even hungrier for success. We like to call that process "failure clears a path for success."

Take, for example, a man who didn't seem to be able to do anything right. He attended school only intermittently as he was growing up, but he was highly ambitious. As a young man he ran for a local general assembly, but lost that election. After that he enlisted in the military where he was assigned to a rifle company and achieved the rank of captain. Unfortunately his company disbanded soon after, forcing him to re-enlist as a private and sending him back to square one.

After serving in the military, he returned home to work in a store that quickly went out of business. He decided to buy his own store, taking on the financial burden with a partner. That also failed, leaving him deeply in debt. His partner died a year later, leaving him responsible for the entire failed enterprise and doubling his debt. The following year this poor man's lifelong sweetheart died and he had a nervous breakdown.

After he recovered from the breakdown, he ran for U.S. Congress. Unfortunately, he lost that election, too. He tried again and was elected to the state legislature, but he declined that seat in order to run for the U.S. Senate, a race which he subsequently lost. He was then nominated to run as the candidate for Republican senator from his home state, but he lost the election after a stunning and now famous (and humiliating) public debate with his opponent.

"Develop success from failures. Discouragement and failure are two of the surest stepping stones to success."

—*Dale Carnegie*

Honestly, this person sounds like a real loser, doesn't he? Did he ever win anything at all? Do you know who we're talking about here? It's Abraham Lincoln (fig. 5–2). He's widely recognized as one of, if not *the*, most successful presidents of all. He helped form our country and hold it together through some of its toughest trials. Think about the Gettysburg Address or the Emancipation Proclamation, two of the most influential and inspirational public statements in history. What did we say before? Great leaders can inspire their followers. Abraham Lincoln was one of the most inspirational speakers ever. He forged through his defeats. His early failures made him strong enough to keep an entire country from ripping itself apart.

Great leaders can inspire their followers.

Fig. 5–2. Abraham Lincoln, 16th president of the United States

LOMBARDI AND HALAS

Vince Lombardi and George Halas were football coaches during the same era in Green Bay and Chicago, respectively. When you watched them, they both spent a lot of time barking at players, and referees; however, they had vastly different leadership styles.

While being interviewed during an ESPN Classics show, when the players from that era were asked to describe the differences between Lombardi and Halas, those who played for the Bears said they would usually receive few rewards after winning a championship, while players from the Packers said they got new cars and their wives got mink coats. Lombardi took care of his players, which made them really like him.

More importantly, the players said they didn't want to disappoint Lombardi. With Halas, they were scared to screw up because they knew they'd get chewed out. With Lombardi, the guys genuinely cared what he thought about them and they didn't want to let him down. This is similar to our "working" officer and lazy lieutenant. The lazy lieutenant didn't inspire his firefighters to work hard, so they would just do the bare minimum necessary to stay out of trouble. That's why their firehouse was a mess and nobody really cared. The working officer, on the other hand, had firefighters following him around the firehouse hanging on his every word.

Surely you've seen the same thing in your experience at various firehouses. Some company officers set very high standards. They want the tools cleaned every shift. Not every day or every week, but *every single shift!* They may not need it at all. Those tools are only getting cleaned because the officer has exacting standards. We all know officers like that. They want you to drill every day, clean the tools every shift. They want the meal to start at exactly 1200 hours and to finish no later than 1230. They want to spend the afternoon doing building inspections and checking hydrants.

Sometimes that type of person can seem like the hardest to work for. They make you toe the line, as opposed to the laid-back officer who says, "Aww, don't worry about it, folks. They'll give us a raise in three years no matter how hard we work. Just hang out and watch some TV. Who cares if we clean the rig? We can still put out fires with a dirty rig, right?"

Is that the kind of officer you really want to work for? Sure, there's not as much work, but you won't learn anything except how to be a lazy firefighter, just like your boss. It was the same thing with Lombardi: If you played for him, you were in for hard work. He set high standards, but it was rewarding to work for someone like him. Most firefighters out there don't want to just coast by; they want to work in the best company for the best officer.

Most firefighters out there don't want to just coast by; they want to work in the best company for the best officer.

A friend of mine, Pete Lund, died several years ago. Pete was a fire lieutenant when I was a firefighter on Rescue 3 (fig. 5–3). I went on to become a lieutenant and captain, and had the pleasure of commanding at several fires where Pete reported to me with the members of Rescue 3.

Fig. 5–3. FDNY Lt. Pete Lund

Pete was a "Lombardi" type of boss. I can still remember when I worked under Pete. I remember pulling up to Rescue 3 and seeing his Long Island Volunteer Fire Chief's car parked outside. Whenever I saw that car I'd always say to myself, "All right! Pete's working today. That means I'm going to have one of the inside positions on the irons, and it's going to be a great tour. We're going to train and do this and that; it's going to be great!"

That was, for me, the Lombardi experience. That was a place where I loved going to work because of my boss. Pete had high standards. The work level was very high in his firehouse, but the fun level was very high, too.

Sure, the hours were tough, but it created a great atmosphere. Here was a guy whose great leadership skills had attracted other quality individuals into his realm. Pete was a hard worker, and that rubbed off on his entire company. You need to know that. As a fire service leader, whether you are a company officer or a chief, know that you are setting the standard. Your people will model their behaviors, habits, and principles based on how you perform.

RUDY!

Let's look back at Rudy Giuliani for a second. Do you remember who Rudy Giuliani was on September 10, 2001?

A lame duck mayor.

What does lame duck mean? See ya! We don't even care what you think because you're not going to be around much longer. He was nearing the end of his second term and wouldn't be allowed to run for a third. There was a mayoral election coming up and he wasn't involved beyond backing one candidate or the other. In other words, he was pretty ineffective. On top of all that, he wasn't exactly depicted as a friendly guy. He was a former federal prosecutor who had gone after the Mafia, so obviously he wasn't a cuddly character before becoming mayor.

As mayor, he was pretty hard nosed, although many people felt he helped the city somewhat (fig. 5–4). Most would say that he had done a decent job, but nobody was writing any books about Rudy Giuliani. At least not on September 10, 2001.

Fig. 5–4. New York City Mayor Rudy Giuliani (second from left) and Fire Commissioner Tom Von Essen (far left) breaking ground on a fire department training facility in December of 2000. Also pictured in uniform is Peter Ganci, a well respected leader who lost his life on 9/11 while serving as FDNY chief of department.

Then what happened? Suddenly we had this gigantic tragic event; a national catastrophe.

What did Giuliani do? He went to the scene of the incident. He was on duty in the city that morning. He wasn't downtown, but he went to ground zero. We've all seen pictures of him walking through the streets with the police and fire commissioners, all three wearing masks and covered in dust. He was almost crushed by one of the buildings that collapsed after Towers One and Two fell.

It was dangerous, but he recognized the gravity of the situation and he went down there to be with the New Yorkers who were working and dying during the largest terrorist attack on American soil. From that day on he had at least one daily press conference, telling people all over the city and country what was going on.

They called him "America's mayor" for a long time after that. He may not have been the most successful person before that day, but he rose to the occasion. He did a great job under stressful, negative conditions, just like Dwight Eisenhower did, like Abraham Lincoln did, and like a lot of other great leaders do. When you're piloting a ship on a stormy sea, sometimes negative conditions can lead to positive outcomes.

★★★★★★★★

When you're piloting a ship on a stormy sea, sometimes negative conditions can lead to positive outcomes.

★★★★★★★★

Colin Powell is one of my idols. I've had a lot of mentors, but he's incredible. He could be giving an eight-hour lecture on tying your shoes and I'd be right there in the front row with a pad and pencil.

I started following him during Desert Storm. First I read his book *My American Journey*. Then I bought the audio version and loved the fact that it was narrated by Colin Powell himself! My idol, talking to me! But talk about perseverance? This guy is the walking, talking definition of the word (fig. 5–5). His entire life is an incredible story of perseverance. Then I found another book written about him, a fantastic book on leadership called *The Leadership Secrets of Colin Powell*. Next to John's book, that may be one of the best books on leadership I've ever read.

Fig. 5–5. General Colin Powell

I was amazed at how much useful information I found in this book. Every page I'd find another thing I could relate directly to what we were doing in the firehouse.

If Colin Powell ran for president tomorrow, I'd have a thousand signs in my yard supporting him. He truly embodies the terms loyalty and integrity.

MEN AREN'T THE ONLY TOUGH LEADERS

All we've talked about up until now are male leaders, but don't kid yourself, men aren't the only effective leaders. There are plenty of women out there who can inspire and lead as well as any man. When you think of Colin Powell, who would be his female equivalent? Former Secretary of State Condoleezza Rice (fig. 5–6). She is one of the most brilliant women ever to serve in the U.S. government.

During her confirmation hearings, you could tell that the senators grilling her were going to try to make some political points by going on the attack. Here's a little woman who they can beat up on in order to look tough, right? Wrong!

She got right up in their faces, challenging every last one of those politicians. She shut down two or three senators completely. No shouting, no insults, just an incredibly intelligent leader shutting down some of the "cave people" out there. We've often told our daughters, if you're looking for a role model, one who embodies the kind of leadership traits, success, and intelligence that you'd like to see in yourself one day, look to Condoleezza Rice.

Fig. 5–6. Condoleezza Rice

REMEMBER WHERE YOU CAME FROM

You hear a lot of the same phrases when people are talking about good leaders. They get things done. They take the lead. They make things happen. They support the team. Another one you hear all the time is, "They remember where they came from."

What does that mean, to remember where you came from? It means that you remember what it was like when you were coming up through the ranks. It means you have empathy for those now going through the same process, because you've been there. You lived it and wore out the t-shirt. That doesn't necessarily mean you have to do everything just like the officers you worked under did it. You may have had one of those strict officers who made you keep the TV off from seven to five, wouldn't let you all go shopping for the shift meal, or wouldn't let you wash your car at the firehouse.

It means you have empathy for those now going through the same process, because you've been there.

We're not saying that's the right way or the wrong way to do things. Sometimes people respond to discipline. What we are saying is that you have to remember how you felt when you were a firefighter, when you were a lieutenant, when you were a captain. Remember what the conditions were like; remember the things you liked and the things you didn't like; remember what was considered acceptable behavior and what wasn't.

You have to remember all those things because all your experiences are going to play a part in your decision-making process. Those experiences are what shape and form your leadership skills. You're not going to do things the way everybody else did them. We're not saying that you have to do things the way your lieutenant did them. You need to do things the way *you* think they should be done, based on the experiences that you've had.

There are some firefighters who make chief, then go around to every firehouse and every station saying, "No television! I didn't have TV so you're not having TV. I wasn't allowed to wash my car during the day so you're not washing your car during the day, either." That's not remembering where you came from, that's just continuing the same old set of rules. That guy is carrying on the same restrictions that he hated, and he probably doesn't even know why. He may not even have any idea why the rule was implemented in the first place. It may have started three administrations before his.

Remembering where you came from just means thinking back to the way things were when you were coming up. If you remember the way things were, then you should be able to make good decisions about the way you want things to be. You don't always have to do things the old way. You could have hated a policy, and you want to do things the exact opposite once you're in command. The point is, you have to use your experience and your judgment to be the best leader you can be.

In my battalion in the Bronx, there are four chiefs. I'm the battalion commander—the senior chief—and there are three other battalion chiefs assigned there. We basically have a four-platoon system so generally, any day of the week, one of the four of us is working.

It's almost like four separate fire departments. The people in my department know that when Chief Salka is working, there are some things they can do and some things I won't let them get away with. They know what I like and what I don't like. I'm sure it's the same way in your firehouse. You have captains or lieutenants who value different things. Some chiefs are sticklers for cleanliness. They want the firehouse to be spotless whenever they stop by. Other officers want the rigs to always be clean, but they're not so worried about the firehouse. I'm sure you have a uniform stickler in your department. Every department has an officer who is considered nitpicky when it comes to uniforms. Some chiefs can't stand fish for the firehouse meal—you get the idea.

I'm the same way. There are some things I'm always on top of and there are other things I could care less about. The firefighters who work under me know what those things are. They know where I'll allow some leeway and where they have no wiggle room at all with me.

Each chief, each company officer, each department is different. As long as you remember where you came from, you can use those experiences to form your own values and priorities. You may have had a positive experience that you want to repeat with the team you lead. You may have had negative experiences that you want to be sure your subordinates don't have to repeat. The priorities you build up over years of experience will be the ones you demonstrate when you're on the job.

Remembering where you came from allows the people who work for you—the ones doing all the work while you're standing at the command post—to realize that you're human. It shows them that you know what's going on because you used to be the one out there pulling hose, putting water on the fire.

WE'RE ALL HUMAN

A lot of departments have rules against doing outside business while you're on a shift. We've both got the phone call before: "Yeah, I'm looking for the guy who paints houses." Lots of firefighters have side jobs. What are you supposed to say? "I can't talk to you right now," and slam the phone down? The public trusts us, and that goes for side work as well. We don't want it to be a disruption, but we understand that those side jobs help put food on a lot of tables and money in college funds. We've both had side jobs. It comes with the territory.

We have both sat on panels for chief's assessments many times. The city manager will give you the job profile, detailing what they're looking for. We sit in on the interviews, too. But the most interesting part is when we get to interview the troops. Time and time again, when we ask the regular firefighter what they're looking for in the next chief, they'll say, "We want a chief who knows the operational side as much as the administrative side. We want a chief who will show up at a fire every once in a while."

You'd be amazed how big a difference the little things make. We've seen more chief officers ruin the relations of their entire department over the smallest piece of equipment. Before you make a bunch of enemies over a tool or a helmet, decide if it's worth it. Ask yourself is that the hill I want to die on? When it's a safety issue, some battles are worth fighting, and you may make some people mad. When it's just an issue of preference, you might consider letting some things go. Your firefighters will be happier and they'll like you better, and that makes doing business much easier and more successful.

Some chiefs just forget where they came from. Some of the chiefs who are making everybody mad would have been at that kitchen table way back when they were firefighters screaming about doing things better if they had the chance and say. Those chiefs have forgotten where they came from and they become disconnected with the troops. As soon as that happens, their ability to lead has become significantly diminished.

Figure 5–7 is a great picture of a fire. Do you have any idea where that incident took place? That was a five-story multiple dwelling in the Bronx. The fire is heavily involved on at least two floors and threatening the exposures on each side, as well as the cockloft.

How many leaders do you think there need to be at that scene? There were three engines, two trucks, and a chief at this fire. Could there be six leaders on this scene? Are there any firefighters here who could be in leadership positions? At our presentations, somebody always says, "The nozzleman!" That's true. When it comes to decisions about when to open the nozzle and where to place the stream, they're the one making that decision. What we're wondering is how many firefighters are out there on their own, with no company officers around them? One example of that would be the roof firefighter. Not every department may have this position, but in the FDNY, we have "roof firefighters." One firefighter from the first truck and one firefighter from the second truck are assigned the roof position.

On a job like the one pictured, there would be two roof firefighters on top of that fire building. The roof position has very delineated assignments, positions, and tools. Neither one of those firefighters would be an officer. They're just firefighters off the first two trucks, two firefighters working remotely from their officer, making decisions and getting the job done. There's never any chain of command there, but one of them will temporarily rise to a leadership role. One firefighter who takes charge says, "Make the hole right here," and that's where they cut. There's no discussion. No argument. One of those regular firefighters rises to the occasion and takes control of that roof. When making those decisions, that person a leader on that fireground.

Fig. 5–7. Fire scene in the Bronx

As soon as the roof has been ventilated, the firefighter relinquishes that leadership role. He or she may head down to the top floor to rejoin the company and help with search efforts. At that point, the person becomes just another firefighter, but while calling the shots on the roof, that firefighter was in a leadership position. There are instances like that all around every single incident.

Officers fill the role of leader all day. Every minute of every incident, they're going to be in leadership positions. And, there are several different layers of leadership during fires and emergencies. It isn't just the incident commander who is the leader at a fire.

Beyond that, there are layers of leadership at the firehouse. There may be one firefighter who makes sure the place stays clean. This person may not be an officer, but just a firefighter who likes things neat and tidy. In that case, he or she is the leader around the firehouse. At a drill, there are layers of leadership. Just giving tips to younger firefighters during training can be a way of showing leadership. The point is, it's not just the officers who can be great leaders. Everyone from the chief down to the volunteer firefighter can act as a leader.

Remember the movie *Titanic*? There's an example of some people who weren't normally leaders stepping up in the face of adversity. As they were lowering the lifeboats into the water, who was in charge of them? It was junior uniformed crewmembers who ended up giving directions. Most of the lifeboats had to be controlled by people who weren't used to being in leadership positions. Some of the boats didn't even have crewmembers to lead them. There were twenty-five or thirty people in a big boat in the middle of nowhere, with no one to lead them. What happened in that case? A passenger rose to the occasion. She stood up and took charge. She said, "You, shut up. You, pick up the oar and start paddling. We're not going that way, we're going this way."

And what did they all do? They went this way.

The people who lead aren't always designated as leaders or those wearing all of the hardware. Sometimes it's just normal people who rise to the occasion. They see an opportunity to help, to do things better, and they seize it. They have something special in them. You can't take a pill to become a leader, and you're not going to find it just lying around. You have to have that special something inside of you.

★★★★★★★★

They see an opportunity to help,
to do things better, and they seize it.

★★★★★★★★

6
GETTING THINGS DONE

Now we're going to take a look at things from the leader's perspective. When it comes down to it, what is your job as a leader? Getting things done. Whether it's the boss, the manager, the supervisor, the lieutenant, or the chief, leaders are expected to finish the job. That's why they're leaders. Although each has a different specific job, finishing the job becomes the basic job description. Each one has a larger group to command, but they are all expected to produce on their respective levels. If things don't get done, then it's on those leaders; however, that doesn't mean they do everything.

THE MVP

Who is the most valuable player in any firehouse? We all have them. It's the firefighter who never sits still. The first one up in the morning. The first one to start washing a dirty rig. When something is broken, that firefighter is right there tinkering with it trying to get it running again. The firefighter at your firehouse who is the most productive is going to be your MVP (fig. 6–1).

But what happens when those firefighters get promoted to lieutenant? They're not washing rigs then. They won't be fixing the tools. They've got whole new levels of responsibility now. They'll be just as enthusiastic as lieutenants as they were as firefighters, but you don't want them down at the firehouse changing oil in their rigs. They have other jobs that they need to do. If they're washing the rigs, then who will be taking care of their responsibilities as lieutenants?

Fig. 6–1. Lewisville (TX) Firefighter Ron Paris is an excellent example of the MVP.

The new lieutenants have to do what Dwight Eisenhower did: delegate. They've got to pass on their old responsibilities to a new round of firefighters. They may have to train some of those younger rookies in how to fix a circular saw or how to wash the rig, but they can't keep doing it for them. That doesn't mean it isn't their job to make sure those things get done.

They've got to pass on their old responsibilities to a new round of firefighters.

They're not allowed to do it themselves, but the lieutenants have to make sure it happens. We've seen it a hundred times, when energetic young firefighters get promoted in a department where they don't provide any mentoring or guidance, they overreach. They try to micromanage and do everything themselves. Sometimes it can be hard to let go of your old habits, but your new leadership responsibilities will suffer if you don't.

"As a leader, your primary job is not
to 'do the work,' but rather to direct,
encourage, support, and develop
the people who do the work. Their
successes are your successes . . .
and their failures are yours as well.
You'll no longer be judged merely
by what you accomplish individually.
Your satisfaction must come from—
and your reputation must be built
on—what your people achieve. You
shine when they are the ones in
the spotlight."

—Steve Ventura

The firefighters are all sitting around the kitchen table, talking and drinking coffee, while the lieutenant is still washing the rig and doing the dishes? Just because he or she did those things for twelve years as a firefighter, it doesn't mean the lieutenant can keep doing them after being promoted; it's ridiculous. On the other hand, if those things don't get done, it's ultimately the lieutenant's fault. If you go to work and something happens at a fire that shouldn't happen, who will take the blame? The company officer. It may not seem right to some, but it's true.

Everything is the company officer's fault: anything that doesn't happen at a fire, but should have; anything that happened too soon, or too late. It might have been a firefighter who screwed up, but the company officer is going to take the blame.

It's the officer's job to make sure that everything gets done in a timely and proper way. If something doesn't get done, then you can bet somebody's going to want to talk to that company officer. We can all agree that our most important asset is our firefighters. Sure our support staff are our favorites, but it's the line firefighter that needs to be taken care of. Our day chiefs, our nine to fivers, are the "stuff-getters." Okay, they set policy, but their job is to support the team. Our battalion chiefs, the shift commanders, are the coaches, but it's the company officers who set that tempo for the shift or that firehouse. They are the go-to people who set the pace. They are in an great position to ensure that things get done right and people stay safe. That's why they carry the added responsibility.

I was working a fire one time, and everybody was pretty exhausted. We had already used all hands, but we needed to do a secondary search in a portion of the building. Since I didn't have any extra units, I grabbed an engine crew that was standing by and available.

"LT, take a couple of guys and head up to the top floor. Give me a secondary search up there and then come back out."

We always want a separate unit to do the secondary search than the one who did the primary. If it's the first search unit, they'll look in the same places and give you the same results. A different set of eyes might catch something the first set missed. We don't normally send engine personnel in to do search, but we do use them on occasion.

I watched the lieutenant and two firefighters walk into the building to do a secondary search, and can you guess what they had in their hands? Nothing. They're engine firefighters. They don't carry tools. There are tools on their rig, but they don't normally carry tools, they carry hose. I put them to work outside their normal routine, and they weren't prepared for it.

As I watched this happen, I was already deciding how I was going to handle the issue. I could have stopped them right there, pointed out their mistake and sent them back to the truck for search tools, but I didn't. Instead I decided to watch and wait.

Ten minutes later I got a call over the radio, "The secondary search is negative on the top floor, chief."

I responded, "Terrific. Come on down."

All three of them came walking out, the firefighters in front followed by the lieutenant. I let the firefighters walk past me and grabbed the officer. "Hang on a minute," I said. "How did your guys do a search without any tools?"

He said, "What? They didn't take any tools?"

"Negative," I responded.

The whole situation ended well. He apologized profusely and said it would never happen again, and I believe him. That's one advantage to delegation. As a chief, you won't have the time to go around making sure every search team uses the proper tools; it's physically impossible. However, you can make sure every lieutenant knows about the importance of search tools. Then you've put the responsibility on their heads.

When we talk about responsibility of leaders, it's understood that they aren't going to do everything. It's the chief's responsibility to make sure that everyone has Halligan tools available, but the chief can't go to every firehouse before every run and make sure all the firefighters bring them along. This can be a very difficult concept to get a hold of for the more enthusiastic, hands-on firefighters. We have pictures of firefighters standing around holding their tools while the captain is cutting a hole in the wall or taking the door.

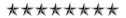

It's the chief's responsibility to make sure that everyone has Halligan tools available, but the chief can't go to every firehouse before every run and make sure all the firefighters bring them along.

You want to grab those captains and say, "Hey! Let your people do that. It's *their* job. Your job is to supervise." Lots of them know they should be letting their firefighters do the work, but they have a hard time letting that hands-on part of the job go. When firefighters promote, they often feel like they're being lazy because they're not doing all of the work anymore. You have to explain to them that it's not their job to force doors anymore. Their job is to supervise. If they're forcing the door or cutting the roof, then they aren't supervising, they're not watching their people, keeping them safe. They're not just taking someone else's job, they're neglecting their own. That's when you have to step in and make sure everyone is filling their roles. Not everyone makes the jump from buddy to boss, smoothly.

> "Things changed the moment you accepted a leadership position."
>
> —*Steve Ventura*

The first part is accepting new responsibility. You have to take on all of the jobs and pressures of being a company officer. The second part is letting go of your old responsibilities. You're not a regular firefighter now. You have to let that part of your career go.

The new responsibility that comes with promotion can be a heavy burden. I have personally witnessed how much it can weigh on an otherwise high-quality firefighter.

One night I had the unfortunate experience of visiting an emergency room (ER) because one of our young guys got hurt. He wasn't going to die, but he had sustained some serious injuries. He had fallen through a roof at a fire.

We were a pretty tight-knit family in that firehouse. We all spent birthdays together, confirmations, holidays, all that stuff. We all worked side jobs together. We knew each others' families, so we were all there at the ER waiting on this young firefighter's wife.

I knew the lieutenant who the firefighter was working under pretty well. I watched him staring out those automatic doors, waiting for the firefighter's wife so he could throw his arms around her and give her a big hug. We were like a family, together through the good times and the bad ones. The lieutenant just wanted to do whatever he could to help.

Finally the two doors slid open and the young firefighter's wife came walking through. She walked right up to the company officer and said, "I thought you were supposed to take care of my husband. I thought you were supposed to keep him safe."

Of course, the poor officer looked like he wanted to turn to dust and disappear. It was hard to watch. That turned out to be a career ender for that officer. He wasn't the same after that. His whole attitude and demeanor got worse. He acted almost like an alcoholic or a chemical dependency case, but it had nothing to do with either of those things. It was the responsibility for that young firefighter's life that destroyed him.

One of the responsibilities you accept when you take a promotion is that you are now taking other firefighters' lives in your hands. People usually talk about the fun side of promotions: getting a raise, getting a uniform upgrade, all those things. It's harder to talk about the serious side of becoming an officer. But if you're not willing to take that responsibility seriously, then don't take on the leadership role. Don't ride up in the front seat. Because if you don't take it serious, you'll be the one getting that visit in the emergency room from someone's spouse saying, "I thought you were supposed to keep them safe."

MORE THAN ONE KIND OF BRAVERY

When we're out doing the normal civilian thing, going to soccer games and PTA meetings, people like to stop firefighters and tell us how brave we are. "Man, you're brave! You firefighters crawl into burning buildings. I don't know how you get up the courage to do that," they say. And they're right. It takes a brave person to ignore all your base survival instincts and run into a burning building to save people or their property. That's the bravery that everyone sees. It's on display every time we respond to a major incident. But there's another kind of bravery that fire officers practice every day. It's the bravery required to take responsibility for another firefighter's life.

Nobody wants to be the officer standing in the ER when some injured firefighter's spouse shows up asking why you didn't protect your firefighters. Nobody wants to take that responsibility, but somebody has to. It takes a lot of guts to stand up and be the boss. When somebody needs to accept responsibility, what has usually happened? Something good or something bad?

Something bad.

There's a long line of people waiting to take credit when something goes right or claim a good idea as their own. You'll never have a problem trying to find someone to pin a medal on. On the other hand, when something bad happens, all of a sudden everyone's headed the other direction. It's harder to find someone to take responsibility when things go to hell. Have you ever had to do that? It's not an easy thing to do.

Several years ago an engine company was celebrating an anniversary. They planned a big ceremony. Invitations went out to the commissioner and chief of department. They sent out invitations to every living firefighter who had ever worked there, no matter where they were.

Retired members flew in from other states. They painted the walls, floor, and ceiling in the firehouse in preparation for the big event. They even touched up the apparatus so everything would look really sharp for the event.

They parked the freshly detailed rig outside and set up chairs and a stage inside the firehouse. They were dedicating a big bronze plaque that day. The press was there. Everyone was in dress uniforms. The chief was there, and even the mayor showed up!

The event started off with the Pledge of Allegiance. The captain had decided that he was going to have four of the newest firefighters do the pledge. They were supposed to come in wearing their dress uniforms, stand at the front, and lead the pledge; everyone would then sit down and the event would continue.

These four young firefighters came marching in with their brand new uniforms on, some of them just days into the fire service. For most of them, this was the first time they'd ever even put their dress uniforms on. What I'm trying to tell you is that these were inexperienced young firefighters.

They marched to the front of the room and started to recite the Pledge, and only two of them were saluting. The other two had their hands over their hearts. It was so embarrassing. Everybody was aghast, but they made it through and sat down.

After that, the first guy to speak was a three-star staff chief and a pretty funny guy if you know him. He's got a very dry sense of humor.

He said, "Well, thanks everybody for being here. Now what was up with the Pledge of Allegiance? I have thirty-eight years on the fire department and I have never seen a firefighter put his hand over his heart while the guy next to him was saluting."

Then the next speaker got up there to talk and he made a crack about the Pledge. Meanwhile, these poor guys are just dying in their chairs. They just wanted to disappear.

Next, the captain of the engine stood up to speak. He said the normal stuff, "Thank everyone for coming. I'm glad you could all make it. We've got a great turnout."

Then he did something unexpected. He said, "Before I say anything else, let me stop and talk about the Pledge of Allegiance for minute. I'm the captain here. I'm the company commander. I accept full responsibility for that little snafu that just happened."

He continued, "Those are my four guys. I just picked them this morning. My intention was to meet with them all before they came up here to instruct them in the proper protocol on whether or not to salute. They were only assigned here two days ago. Some of them haven't even worked a shift yet. I haven't even given them a formal tour of the firehouse yet, so let's cut them some slack. I should have discussed with them when to or not to salute but I didn't, so this certainly isn't their fault. As a matter of fact, I think those guys did a great job. Let's give them a round of applause!"

And everybody clapped and those four probies were smiling like they did something right.

I wouldn't have been happy with the captain at the time. That was not a positive thing that just happened in front of the chief and the mayor. It was embarrassing. Still, what he did next that day eventually moved the captain up about a hundred points in my eyes. He stepped up and took responsibility for something that was his fault. He didn't try to lay the responsibility on someone else. He could have said, "I don't know what they're teaching these kids over at the academy."

Instead, he did the right thing. It was his fault. He even went a step further and took the weight off his people by asking for that round of applause. He shouldered that burden, like a good leader should, and made his young firefighters feel less guilty about the mistake.

Now that's taking responsibility for your actions! He could have waited until afterward and pulled the rookies aside and apologized to them, but he stood up in front of the chief, the mayor, and everybody else and took the blame."

EXPERIENCE

Youth definitely has its advantages. As we get older, we all become highly aware of that fact; however, seniority has its advantages as well. With age comes experience. If you have thirty years in the department, there are very few situations that you haven't seen dozens of times. You can pull up to an incident and already know exactly what is going to happen. You've seen smoke that color before. You know what smoke pushing out of those windows is going to do. You can tell by the smell what kind of fire it is. You can smell the difference between rubbish burning in a high-rise's incinerator, a mattress fire, a car fire, a structural fire, food on the stove, and probably a few more to boot.

Experienced firefighters can pull up at a fire and tell you that it's food burning on the stove just by smelling the smoke. They won't even be in the building yet, much less on the fire floor. You can't put a price on that kind of experience. It's the type of thing experienced officers have in their back pockets. They can tell on sight a lot of things that less experienced officers will have to learn the hard way.

Some people will tell you that relying on your young officers is legitimate. We've even said that you have to delegate responsibility to younger officers, and you do. This is different. If you don't have someone in a leadership capacity in front of the building, you can't see what's burning. You can't see where the fire is headed. You can't see what color the smoke is or what it may be telling you about what is burning.

Some people say there's too much confusion at the front of the fire building to run a fire. If there is too much confusion for you on the fireground, you've got a command and control problem. We always refer to a fire scene as organized chaos, but if we're the ones getting excited then we have big problems. They called 9-1-1 for us; we can't call 9-1-2. We're it! You should be able to operate in a little bit of confusion, a little bit of mayhem. It's one thing to get excited, but you have to be able to retain a measure of control in that type of environment. The goal should be to try and act like it's not your first fire (fig. 6–2).

They called 9-1-1 for us;
we can't call 9-1-2. We're it!

Fig. 6–2. The officer with the calm demeanor, who works extremely well under pressure, will find a long list of warriors who will want to follow him into battle. An example is Lewisville Captain Chris Sweet, pictured, now Battalion Chief Sweet, who has that "calm" way of doing business no matter the crisis.

Take a look at figure 6–3. It's a two-story frame house, heavily involved. Who is in charge of this incident? Who is in charge of what's going on at that building?

Fig. 6–3. Who is in charge of this incident?

Take a look at the person in the white helmet—the one out in front of the building. The officer is in a really advantageous position there because two sides of the building are visible. The position was deliberately chosen because that's the best place to see the whole picture. They can give input from that location to those working inside and any other bosses on the scene as to the fire's progress.

Can you make out the firefighter in the second story window? There is no smoke in that room. It's an amazingly clear room, considering the situation. He might report, "Looks good here, chief. No fire on second floor." This chief officer can see what's really going on because he's stationed where he can view the entire scene. That's a fairly extreme example, but you get the idea. If you can't see what's happening, then you might not be getting the whole story. Especially if you don't have those officers in good positions around the building.

You have to learn to take a few steps back as you work your way up the ladder. That chief has taken quite a few steps back over his career. If he were still a lieutenant, he might be in the room with that other firefighter. If he were a captain, he might be somewhere else in the building. Now that he's the chief, he's taken a few more steps back to a spot where he can view the incident as a whole.

When you make battalion chief, district chief, or assistant chief—whatever rank is on your uniform—you have to take a few steps back. You have to leave some of the old job behind and pick up some new parts. Neither one of us has carried a tool in years. We know young chiefs who still carry tools. They have little tools they like to carry with them for comfort. Why point out that they are "young"? It's because they aren't fully chiefs in their own heads yet. They think like they are captains. That's why they carry the tools. They still think they might need them, but they don't. They're chiefs now. Chiefs don't need tools. Chiefs position themselves in front of the fire building or take other command assignments that do not require them to carry tools. You have to mentally make that shift. There are a lot of things that chiefs do that firefighters don't, and vice versa. As you get further away from having those tools in your hands, there are different responsibilities you'll pick up.

You have to leave some of the old job behind
and pick up some new parts.

The other thing you have to realize is that everything that happens at that fire is on that chief. Good, bad, or otherwise, that chief is responsible for what goes on. The chief is not physically doing any actual firefighting, but as the senior officer at that incident is taking on the responsibility for the entire scene. Do you want to know a secret? Neither one of us does much at a fire. We don't touch a tool. We don't cut any holes. We don't drive any rigs. We don't operate any nozzles. We talk on the radio a little bit, but that's about it. A company officer does a whole lot more physically than either one of us would at a fire, but that's how it's supposed to be. Each position has its own level of responsibility.

ACTING RANKS

A lot of departments have what they call "acting ranks." In New York City, if a chief gets injured in the middle of a tour, they take the senior captain and make him or her the acting battalion chief for the rest of the tour. They make the lieutenant into the acting captain, and so on down the line. For the rest of that tour, you've got a firefighter acting as the lieutenant. That person has to let go of the duties of a firefighter and take on the duties of a lieutenant, which is a hard thing to do. We've seen people who have been chiefs for a year or two before they figure that out. They keep trying to do their old jobs and their new ones, too. They need to stop for a second and realize they can't be inside anymore. It is their duty to stay outside and survey the entire scene. If they are inside on a nozzle then there's nobody doing that job and the rest of the firefighters will all suffer for it.

THERE'S NO "RIGHT WAY"

Everyone treats situations differently. If you have ten different chiefs at an incident, you're going to end up with ten different ways to work it. The Lake Cities Fire Department is going to have different policies and procedures than the FDNY. They might let something slide in one department that is a major violation in the Lewisville Fire Department.

The point is that there are a lot of different ways to get things accomplished. You wouldn't want to use wildland tactics at a high-rise fire. Different approaches work better for different departments. How many people do you have on duty or on call? How many chiefs are in your department? Not only the environment in which you work, but the size and makeup of your department will affect how you get things done.

Don't take everything we say in this book as the unquestionable truth. You may do things differently in your department. We've worked together for over half our lives, but there are still areas where the two of us disagree. One thing we will always agree on is that no matter what, there is always a way to get something done, always a way to look at things differently, and always a way to finish the day.

I'm going to tell you a story about a pretty negative event that happened several years ago. Ed Koch was the mayor of New York City, so that should give you some idea the timeline I'm talking about.

It was Super Bowl Sunday, and the mayor closed down a firehouse. There weren't any rules or contracts at the time, and they could just close a firehouse down without any procedure. As a result of the outrage over that incident, they've instituted a 45-day notification requirement if they intend to close a firehouse. At the time, however, no advance notification was given.

There was an absolute uproar: 5,000 firefighters marched over the Brooklyn Bridge in protest. It was a terrible time for the FDNY. Negative, us-against-them attitudes were pervasive in the department.

About three months after that closing, things were still tense. There was a promotion ceremony and Assistant Chief Lou Harris was in charge. He had about thirty-seven years on the job at the time. He was running the promotion ceremony because the chief was out of town.

I was up for promotion, along with a bunch of other firefighters. I'd worked in a study group of about five guys for that promotion test. We met up at each other's houses once a week for what seemed like three years leading up to the test. We all knew each other well and we were pretty good buddies.

Assistant Chief Harris stood up there and gave the usual speech. "Congratulations to you all. To the fine lieutenants and captains, you're going to be the new bosses and leaders in this fire department." It was the standard promotion speech.

Then he broke from tradition and addressed the current situation. "I want to advise you all not to worry too much about what's going on right now. There's a lot of turmoil, a lot of hate, and a lot of bad feelings about what happened with that company being closed. You have to let that go and take care of your problems. Take care of your platoon. The five or six people who are working under you, make sure they're well-trained and happy. Don't get dragged down by these other negative issues, just ignore it and pay attention to your little piece of the world."

No one in the audience at the time could believe it. I thought, "What's he saying? Ignore it? What they did was wrong for New York and it was wrong for the fire department!" I was incensed at what he was saying. We all were.

Only years later did I realize that he was absolutely right that day. I tell my firefighters that same thing all the time. "Don't worry about it. Focus on yourselves. Dealing with this is my job." It all goes back to responsibility. The younger members aren't responsible for administrative-level decisions, so it doesn't make any sense for them to waste time arguing about them.

I changed my opinion drastically from when I was a firefighter going through his first promotion. You'll change a lot as you work your way up the ranks, too.

Sometimes you have to disconnect yourself somewhat from your department as a whole. You may think your chief is an idiot who couldn't make a good decision if lives depended on it. Who cares? Does the chief do anything that really affects the daily operation of your firehouse? Of course his or her decisions affect your life in a broad way, but there is very little a fire chief does that will affect the day-to-day operations in a firehouse.

Instead, focus on your firehouse. Your department may be falling down around you, but you can still have a happy, well-trained firehouse in spite of whatever else is going on, no matter what rumors are flying about closings or downsizing. Do what you can to make your firehouse a positive place to work every day.

YOUR OWN LITTLE WORLD

No matter what level you're at, firefighter or battalion chief, you need to keep your focus on the things you can control. As a chief, you have to be able to say, "I don't really care what my deputies are doing. As long as I'm not getting complaints and they're doing the right thing, then I'm happy." You'll see them at fires every once in a while, but other than that, you have to accept the fact that they are doing their jobs—you trust them.

The same idea works at headquarters, too. If you're a lieutenant, then it's your job to keep your company happy. If you're the chief, then it's your job to keep headquarters happy. Just work on your own little world. You can't make much of a difference outside of it, so there's no reason to waste time worrying about it. If you keep what's going on in your little realm friendly, effective, and productive, then you'll be a happier firefighter. Keep the positive energy flowing and you'll draft more into that circle. Sooner or later, you'll start to affect things outside your little world and all just by concentrating on the things you can fix, and not the things you can't. Use your energy wisely! Don't waste it.

It all comes back to team building. Every now and then you need to worry about your team and allow the rest of the department to take care of themselves. Your team is made up of the people who work immediately around you. If you're the chief, then obviously your team is the entire department; however, you can't worry about every single firefighter. You have to focus on building a good team around you, and letting those in the leadership positions below you lead and develop those in their charge.

If you could build the perfect team, who would you want to put on it? Lots of people would say, "Ten more firefighters just like me!"

In some cases we can't take the one of you now, so forget it. Not only that, but it would be a pretty lousy team. When you look at a truly good team, you'll notice that its members aren't all perfect. Whether you're talking about work or sports, the best teams have a wide range of diversity. The individuals may not be the best at what they do, but each has something to offer. Each is probably better at something than everyone else on that team. They come from different backgrounds, different education levels, and different upbringings, which gives them each a unique viewpoint on every incident.

We discover talents all the time in our people that we didn't know they had. We're all firefighters, but you'll find that one firefighter in your company who may also be a mason. Another firefighter works as an electrician in a side job. Another one might speak a different language that could come in handy on a call. When you take all those talents and put them together, you get a pretty solid team that's ready for just about any problem that comes their way.

The reason they're going to be so effective is their diversity. When you have a variety of people, you can make use of their varied individual backgrounds to improve the team as a whole. You just have to be willing to shut up and listen. Sit down with the people in your company and learn what special skills they have. "Everybody here is a firefighter. What makes you stand out? What else do you bring to the table?"

We don't just do firefighting; we all have lives outside of the firehouse. Your job as a leader is to harness all those skills and blend them together to make them work for you. We prefer to hire people with those extracurricular activities. If you're a plumber or an electrician for your side job, you bring more to the table than a kid who just got out of the academy and doesn't know anything about the world other than what he or she learned in class.

You probably have firefighters in your company right now with skills you don't know about. Talk to your human resources department and have them send out a questionnaire asking firefighters to list their other talents. Find out how many members are nurses or paramedics, how many do construction work, how many are electricians. Look for all the other talents you have in the department aside from just passing Firefighter I and II. Once you start to find everybody's talents, you will see that it increases positive results. You will begin to see how having a diverse team can greatly improve your entire work experience.

First off, they'll improve your experience on the fireground. How many times have you come across a fire of some sort of electrical components? How much easier is it to solve that issue if there's a certified electrician on your team? Another advantage you'll glean from this process is an increase in team unity and trust. The people working under you will feel appreciated when you talk to them about their other skills. It will make them feel more useful when they can bring those talents to bear at an incident. When an electrician is called on to find the breaker box and cut the power, that person is the star for the moment.

Not only that, but when one person steps up and goes above and beyond the ordinary, it inspires the other people around them to do the same. The entire company wants to do more, to overachieve—to be better firefighters. Identifying special skill sets can also improve your effectiveness at incidents. If you already know who is an electrician in your company, you don't have to waste time asking around when you really need one. You just turn to the fire-fighter who can do the job and say, "Get going!" There is no hesitation. In our line of work, a few seconds can mean the difference between life and death. That way you work like a well-oiled machine instead of a bunch of ducks wandering around in a thunderstorm.

That way you work like a well-oiled machine instead of a bunch of ducks wandering around in a thunderstorm.

You can really see the difference when you get detailed out for the day and go to a place where they don't have much unity or trust. When people are familiar with one another, the entire team works more smoothly because everyone knows each other's skills. Some departments like to rotate their officers. Some like to rotate all their company officers every two or three years. If you're a company officer, you may never spend more than two or three years in any single firehouse. On the one hand, that can be an advantage because it allows you to vastly increase your network. In a rotation system like that, you're going to come in contact with more people. On the other hand, you're never really going to develop that team unity. About the time a company starts to build up a level of trust with their officer, he or she is transferred to another firehouse.

A lot of people talk about building a quality team, but they don't know where to start. There are a million things we could say about team building, but the best advice is to understand the process. A lot of people will assemble a team and think the job is done, but coming together is just the beginning. The harder, second step is keeping that group together. Not only do you need to know what each person's skill set contains, you also need to be able to manage their egos. Even without meaning to do it, people will step on each other's toes. Some people don't take criticism very well. There are a whole lot of personality problems that can arise to destroy team unity.

> "Coming together is a beginning.
> Keeping together is progress.
> Working together is success."
>
> —*Henry Ford*

If you're able to make it through that part of the process, you'll start to achieve success. If you're able to discern your team members' individual talents and hold them together, everyone will enjoy team success. That, in turn, will build more unity, which will lead to more success. That includes the "unofficial" leaders. When new firefighters come to a company, and all those firefighters gather around them, showing them tricks and telling them the ground rules, that's the entire team building unity.

The team absorbs new members and brings them up to speed. They tell them when they should get there early, when they need to work a funeral, when they need to help out around the firehouse, all the things that will help them to become productive members of the team. Every member of that team bears responsibility to keep it running smoothly.

7
INTEGRITY

As much as we've tried to make this a complete book on leadership, it certainly doesn't have all the answers. This book only contains information that we've learned over two careers in the fire service. There are a lot of lessons out there that we don't know about or have yet to learn ourselves. Furthermore, this book has grown out of some much smaller projects. We've taken bits and pieces from different life experiences we've had and added them in. There are lessons we learned 20 years ago and lessons we learned last week mixed throughout this book.

We are trying to make it as complete as possible. It certainly doesn't contain everything you'll ever need to know about leadership because we don't know everything there is to know on the subject. Even though they all may be a little bit different, one of the things that will probably come up in any lesson on leadership is integrity.

What is integrity? Is it the willingness to do what you know to be right even if it isn't what everyone around you wants you to do? *Doing what you know is right.* That's a pretty good definition of integrity—short and to the point. It's not what anyone else thinks. It's not what everyone else wants to see or do. It's doing what you know to be right, even if it goes against everyone around you. You won't have to wait long to find out if the people around you think you're making bad decisions. The firehouse isn't a place where you find a lot of nonsense. Firefighters say what they mean. If your people think you're doing the wrong thing, you *will* hear about it.

*What is integrity? Is it the willingness
to do what you know to be right even if it isn't
what everyone around you wants you to do?*

That brings up another point about integrity: You have to follow through. You can't say one thing and then do another. Firefighters are a vocal bunch. If you don't follow through on what you've told your team, then you're going to have problems. You have to say what you mean, but if your actions don't back that up then nobody will listen to you. Your message and your actions have to be consistent. If you say one thing in the firehouse, but do something different at an incident, you lose all your credibility. Pretty quickly, your members will stop listening to you because they've learned you're full of it.

"As a leader, you have to not only do the right thing, but be perceived to be doing the right thing. A consequence of seeking a leadership position is being put under intense public scrutiny, being held to high standards, and enhancing a reputation that is constantly under threat."

—*Jeffrey Sonnenfeld and Andrew Ward*

It's important that you don't just preach about integrity, but show it. If your firefighters see that what you say matches what you do, then they're going to respect you. They know that their captain isn't just full of hot air, but can back it up! That type of integrity is one of the cornerstones of leadership. Without it there probably won't be anyone who wants to follow your lead.

PRACTICE WHAT YOU PREACH

Lots of people talk about integrity, but when it comes to actually acting with integrity they fall woefully short. It's acting with integrity that makes people believe in a leader. It has to do with honesty, both with yourself and those around you. If you're not honest with the people around you, then you won't be a very effective leader. If you act with honesty and integrity, then those same people will follow you into a burning building without a second thought (fig. 7–1). Integrity is a pretty powerful thing, when you think about it.

Fig. 7–1. FDNY Lt. Billy Butler (far left) with his crew from 56 Truck. Lt. Butler is a great example of a leader who has integrity. The result? His firefighters will follow him anywhere.

You have to truly believe in what you're saying. One of our buddies has a saying that goes, "Just because I sleep in my garage every night doesn't make me a car." Integrity is so high on our list because none of the rest of this information means a thing without it. If you don't have integrity, you might as well throw this book away. You can read the rest of the points we make in this book, and they're all good points, but if you have no integrity then you won't be able to implement them effectively. You can have the best tactical mind in the world, but if your firefighters don't believe in what you say, it won't matter a bit on the fireground.

You can have the best tactical mind in the world, but if your firefighters don't believe in what you say, it won't matter a bit on the fireground.

Integrity is one of, if not *the*, biggest foundations necessary to be an effective leader, both in and out of the fire service. For example, take firefighters who are consistently late for their shifts. They always call ahead of time to let you know they're running late, so technically they are following procedure. You've told your people that it's okay to be a bit late if they have to, but be sure to call and let someone know about it. Just because they aren't breaking any of the big rules doesn't mean they're pulling their weight. They are following the letter of the law, but not the spirit. That rule is in place so that someone doesn't get written up if they have an emergency, but these firefighters are using it as an excuse to avoid fulfilling their obligations. Eventually you will have to pull these firefighters aside and have a talk with them.

"What's the deal with you being late all the time? It's three or four times in a row now that you've been late. I know you're calling ahead, but that doesn't excuse it when it's happening all the time. If you come in late again, I'm going to have to write you up." Lots of normal firefighters are going to take the hint and fall in line. Every once in a while, you'll get someone who just can't get it together. When that happens, you have to stand by what you said. If you said you were going to write this person up, you have to do it. This person may be well liked. He or she may come to you and say, "This time *really* was an emergency. My spouse was sick and I had to pick up the kids from school. I'm awful sorry. It won't happen again."

What should you do in that situation? You have to say to the firefighter, "That's tough." You don't have to be mean about it. You can say it nice or you can say it firm, whatever your personal style and the situation warrant. It doesn't matter how you say it. The point is that you said last time, "One more time and you're going to get docked." Now you *have* to dock the firefighter. Otherwise, your word means nothing. We refer to it as "using up your coupons," or in other words, a "get out of jail free" card. That firefighter has used up all the coupons. You're not being a hard-nosed lieutenant by holding to this. Everybody starts off with a few coupons, because stuff happens. We realize that life doesn't go perfect and sometimes things will come up. In those cases, we're more than willing to cut a hard working firefighter a break.

It's a lot like Eddie Enright and the "working officer." That lieutenant hadn't used up all his coupons. He had been doing the right things the right way all along. Because of that, he could cash in one of his coupons when his uniform wasn't up to code. You don't want to come down like a ton of bricks on someone the first time. The person probably has a valid reason to be late. When it happens over and over again, and you have to ding somebody to get his or her attention, chances are, the person's coupons are probably used up.

It's similar to parenthood. If you tell your kid, "You're gonna get it!" but nothing ever happens, then eventually the kid will realize there are no consequences for bad actions. Not only will the child realize it, but any other kids in your family will learn the same lesson. It's no different in the firehouse. If that firefighter comes in late repeatedly and you don't do anything about it, the other members of your team will notice. You may have pulled the late-arriving firefighter aside and had a private chat with the warning, "One more time and you'll be written up." You may have been very discreet so as not to embarrass the firefighter in front of the troops. Even so, the other people in the firehouse *will* find out what was said. They *will* know that you've given that firefighter an ultimatum. If that person shows up late again, they *will* know it. More importantly, they *will* know that you didn't keep your word. It's the first step in watching your word crumble along with your integrity.

"We are watching everything you do. Even when you think we're not paying attention, we are. There is never a time when you're not in your leadership role. You may think that when you choose to ignore an issue, you are not leading. You're wrong! We get the message. If you show up late for a meeting, you lead us to believe that our time isn't valuable. If you lose your cool and overreact to small issues, we wonder how you will react when something big comes along. It's a fact; you are always leading. You can never not lead! Everything you do counts!"

—*David Cottrell*

Little cracks like that can be the demise of your integrity. You could be a wonderful officer otherwise. Everyone likes you. You are a good tactical fire officer; however, none of that will matter if your firefighters don't respect you. You might not always make the popular choice, but if you always make what you believe is the right decision, then your people will respect you for it.

★★★★★★★★

None of that will matter
if your firefighters don't respect you

★★★★★★★★

COLLAPSE

Integrity can be something that is slowly worn away by little chips like the situation above, but it can also come crashing down very quickly. You could have been in the department for fifteen years, known by your fellow officers for walking the straight and narrow, looked up to for your impeccable integrity; yet you make one misstep in judgment and it will all come crashing down.

Once integrity is gone, it's gone. You can't just wash it, dry it out, and then put it back on. Once it's broken, you may never get it back. Integrity is something that takes a long time to build and must be maintained with vigilance, yet it can be destroyed in a single moment. That's why it's so precious. You're either an honest person or you're not. Just like you can't be half-pregnant, you can't be half-honest. Your character is built by integrity. One of the best ways to define your character is by how you act when no one else is in the room. When there's no one there to impress or "apple polish," how will you act?

A good example: Think of a department that has been giving public CPR classes for thirty years. For three decades, they've been teaching basic life-saving techniques to anyone who wanted to learn. I think we can all agree that's an admirable achievement. Still, if that department has one negative incident it can wipe out thirty years of good community relations. Those types of negative incidents will follow you and your department. How many times have you asked about a department only to hear something like, "Didn't those guys burn down five houses in a row one time?" It turns out that incident was 26 years ago, but that's still what people think about when you mention that place.

The point is, once you give up your integrity, you really have nothing else. It takes a long time to gain back people's trust. It's hard for people to trust each other with little things, let alone their lives. That's why we won't allow thieves or liars in our firehouse. If you lie, if you steal, we will do everything possible to get you out of our firehouse. If you can't be trusted in the firehouse, how can you be trusted once that bell goes off?

Once you give up your integrity,
you really have nothing else.

People who lack integrity are the ones who will leave you in a burning building. Lots of firefighters have had people leave them. We've both been left and we can still remember the person who did it. That's why integrity is so important in our profession. It's impossible to do your job correctly if you don't trust the other people on your team. The same thing goes for you as a leader. If your firefighters can't trust you, then you won't be an effective leader. That's why you have to be conscientious and maintain your integrity at all times. You may never be able to get it back once you lose it. It's better just to never let it get away from you in the first place.

There are a lot of things you can be pretty good at doing. You can be a pretty good ballplayer. You can be pretty good with cars. You can be pretty good with tools. One thing you can't be pretty good at is honesty.

No one has ever said, "He's pretty honest. You know, he's okay at being honest."

You know why no one has ever said that? Because it doesn't exist. Either you're honest or you're not. You can't be in the middle. I know we've said there isn't always a black-and-white answer in the fire service, but in this case that's how it is. There is no middle ground with honesty.

How important is honesty to the firehouse? Do you lock your door when you aren't in your office? Do you have locks on your personal lockers? Do you use them?

I've got 33 years in the fire department and I've never locked my locker or my office. Some days I may only have two bucks in my pocket, other days $200.

I take that back, at one point we had to lock our lockers because homeless people used to come in and go through our things while we were out on a call. I've never ever locked it out of the fear of a fellow firefighter, though. That's a sign of the trust that exists in my firehouse.

The door to my office is always open, never locked. The door to my locker is never locked. I have pictures of my kids inside the locker. My pants are hanging there with my money in the right pocket. We've had break-ins once in a while, but in general I just don't worry about it.

I've left my wallet just sitting out at the firehouse before. I've left my watch behind after a shift, too. You know what happens every time? Someone comes up to me on the next shift and says, "Hey, John. I found your wallet."

Either that or there will be a note or a message from someone saying, "John, your wallet is in your drawer." Those are just two examples of the trust that exists where I work.

Obviously we're a lot more familiar with the people we work around, but the point is that we have a higher level of trust at the firehouse. Someone who works at the bus depot wouldn't just leave a wallet out and expect to get it back. Do you think a supermarket clerk would really expect to get a watch back if it was left sitting on a shelf next to the cereal boxes?

If that happens, that's wonderful; however, I doubt too many would take the risk. Firefighters, on the other hand, have a higher level of trust in their profession than most. It's necessary on the fireground, but it starts back in the firehouse. If I can't trust you with my watch, then I'm not going to trust you with my life.

When things are going your way, it's easy to be "the good guy." If you aren't having any problems, then it's very easy to be completely honest. It's not hard to tell your troops they're doing a fantastic job. Everybody loves to let their people know it when they do well.

The hard part comes when things aren't going your way. It's a lot harder to stand up and speak the truth when you know you're going to get your butt chewed out for it.

I had a firefighter who fell off a ladder. His injuries required surgery. After the surgery, his wounds took forever to heal. He had used up all his sick time as well as his vacation days. He wasn't even working a fire. He was just doing a project on a day off and he fell off of a stepladder and shattered his ankle. The ankle was so bad they were considering amputation.

This was a young firefighter with small children who had run out of time. He was not ready to return to the job, but didn't have any more discretionary days left, so what was he supposed to do?

I knew it wasn't really the department's policy, but I explained how we could cover for this young firefighter. We transferred two or three people over from other firehouses to cover his shifts. We did some creative scheduling and were able to cover all this firefighter's shifts until he was well enough to come back to work.

About six months down the road, I got a call from my boss, and he chewed me out, big time! "You've got a guy who's been out for six months? I want you, and I want your battalion chief both in my office first thing tomorrow!"

Remember, I have a great boss who is a great guy, so I don't want him coming across as mean and uncaring, because he's not. He cares about his employees very much. But he had a right to be upset. He just didn't know all the details.

I told my boss, "Let's leave the battalion chief out of it. This was my deal. I approved it. I even made suggestions as to how the team could work it out. I believe in what we did."

I remember thinking, "Well, I can always get a job somewhere else."

The human resources director, who is incredible, even heard about it and called me up, asking me if I'd been chewed out badly. After that, she worked up a "vacation donation" policy that ended up being used for the entire city so that other employees in that same situation wouldn't face the same problem of not having enough time banked, wondering how they'd put food on the table.

I knew that my decision to help this firefighter out for such an extended period probably wouldn't be liked by the higher-ups. I was aware that I was probably going to get chewed out and maybe even disciplined if they found out. Even so, I wasn't willing to risk that firefighter's future and his family by doing nothing. I knew he was a good firefighter who just had an accident. If he was given time, he would come back and be a good firefighter again; however, if we cut him loose, who knows where he would end up?

In this case, I knew it would be an unpopular decision, but it was the right one. Because I took a stand for this one young firefighter, we devised a system whereby other firefighters could help a brother or sister in need during a similar situation.

Lots of good came out of that decision. Not only did we come up with the vacation donation policy, but my firefighters saw that I was willing to stand up for what I believed was the right thing to do and argue it if needed. When they saw that I had integrity, it did more to make them trust in my leadership than a title ever could. If you stand behind your people, then they will do the same for you.

THE HIGHEST LEVEL OF TRUST

What does the average citizen think about the fire service? Our customers, the people we serve, do they have a positive view of the fire department where you work? If they trust firefighters, then they will love us. When he's asked to define the trust the public has in firefighters, fire service legend Chief Alan Brunacini says, "We're the ones they let cut the pajamas off their granddaughters." What he means by that is the public trusts us. They trust us when the lives of their closest family members are on the line. They trust us when they're at their most vulnerable (fig. 7–2).

Fig. 7–2. Lincolnshire-Riverwoods (IL) Squad Company. That level of trust doesn't just happen to a fire company. It is earned.

There are Fortune 500 companies that would kill for the marketing advantage enjoyed by the American fire service. We may have our own little problems from time to time, but we're still the most trusted uniform in America. Just watch a few minutes of commercials. Everything from hemorrhoid medication to fast food uses the image of the firefighter in their advertisements. Why do so many companies and organizations use the image of a firefighter to symbolize their group? Because we stand for trust. We stand for integrity.

When I first moved from Coeur d'Alene to Lewisville, not many people knew who I was. They didn't need to know—I was the fire chief.

A few weeks after we moved in, there was a knock at our door. My wife answered to our neighbor from across the street. She said, "Hello. You don't know me. I live right down the block there. My husband and I are going away on vacation and the girl we usually have watch our house is unavailable. Do you think you could watch our house?"

My wife said, "Sure. Come on in." As they talked about it, my wife found out why she'd decided to ask us to watch her house.

She said, "I saw the red chief's car in the driveway, so I knew your husband was a firefighter."

Just seeing the red car in the driveway was enough. She was willing to turn over her house keys to someone she'd never met in her entire life. That's the level of trust we're afforded as firefighters.

★ Why do we need integrity?

Do you need integrity to roll a hose? Nope.

Do you need integrity to cut a roof? No.

Do you need integrity to vent a window? Negative.

So why do firefighters need integrity? Because we're there in people's darkest hour. We're there when they get dragged out of their homes unconscious. We're crawling through that burning house, searching for their children.

Have you ever been asked to empty your pockets when you left a house? No. They don't question you, they kiss you. If they questioned you like that, you'd be insulted. You'd say, "What are you talking about? I just risked my life to save your children and you're accusing me of stealing?" We have to maintain that level of integrity if we're going to maintain the image of the fire service. We've all been lucky enough to inherit this amazing relationship with the public from the people who came before us. It's our job to maintain that reputation of integrity. Someday, we will be obliged to pass it on to the folks coming after us, but in the meantime, we have to make sure we don't damage the sterling reputation of the fire service. We've got to live up to that integrity—we have to do what is right.

When I'm at work, I am the battalion commander. That means I'm a battalion chief. I'm not just the battalion chief, I'm a *senior* battalion chief, so I set policy in the battalion and all sorts of other administrative, bureaucratic stuff.

When I am at home, I'm not the battalion chief. Anybody who is married knows what I'm talking about, right? When I'm at home I'm just Dad.

One day I was knocking out a list of things to get done. One of the things on the list was a trip to a home improvement store. When I got out of my truck in the parking lot, the first thing I noticed was a cell phone sitting on the ground. It looked brand new. The battery was still good and screen was functioning when I flipped it open. It was just sitting there and I almost expected someone to come up behind me and say, "Oh, you found my phone. Thanks so much."

It couldn't have been sitting there long or the battery would have been lower. Now I was faced with a decision. I can either take the phone into the store and leave it at the lost-and-found, or I could try to track down the owner myself.

It's likely that it belonged to someone who was inside the store. Still, if the owner had already left, he or she might not be able to identify where the phone had been lost. It could just sit there in the lost-and-found forever.

Because I didn't want to pass off the responsibility, I decided to try to locate the owner myself. This was a brand new phone with lots of numbers in it. Not only would someone be looking for it, but I didn't think it would be too hard to find the owner if I called some of the numbers in the contact list.

Even if your intentions are good, if you turn it over to the manager then you haven't really followed through. The manager might have been fired that day. The manager might not be a very honest person and might need a cell phone. In that case, you handing it in might have been the honest thing to do, but you're not really doing any good. Instead I chose to try to return it myself.

I made a couple of phone calls immediately as I was walking into the store. I only got voice-mail, but I left several messages, providing the location of the lost phone and my number.

I took care of my wife's shopping, got what I needed, then came back out about a half hour later and climbed into my truck. Before I drove away, I made another half dozen calls. I even got somebody to pick up the phone, but the person said, "I'm busy," and hung up on me. I couldn't get anybody to take my calls or call me back.

When I got back home after running my errands, my seventeen-year-old son was sitting at the table eating pizza and cake for breakfast. I laid the shopping bag and the cell phone on the table.

I saw his eyes light up. "Oh, you got a new phone? That's the MX3000!"

He was thinking, "If he got a new phone, maybe I'm getting a new phone, too!"

I explained what had happened and told him I needed to find out who it belonged to and return it. His response was, "Why? They've probably got insurance. Just keep it."

Get the heck out of here! I chased him out of the room. I told him, "I'm not keeping the phone. No matter how you rationalize it, it's still wrong."

Later that same day a buddy of mine calls. He wanted me to come help on some job. I told him I didn't have time, that I had some things to do of my own. Besides that, I still had this cell phone whose owner I was trying to locate.

"What did you find?" he asked me.

"An MX3000 or whatever it's called." I answered.

He said, "Oh, did you know that's compatible with your phone? You can just pull your SIM card and swap them out. Then you can keep that phone."

I had to get rid of him, too, and hung up. All these people were trying to sway me from doing the right thing. You'll find that around the firehouse, too. Some of your best people will beg you to forget about the rules, just this one time. It's tempting, I can tell you.

About an hour after I hung up on my firefighter buddy, I got a call. It was the phone owner's wife. She was so happy that I'd found it. Turns out it was her husband's brand new business phone. He hadn't realized he'd lost it that morning while he was picking up some things at home improvement store. I scheduled a meeting with the woman to get her the phone back.

My daughter came along with me when I went to take the phone back. I met the woman at a gas station maybe fifteen minutes away. I gave her the phone back and she was very appreciative.

I walked back and climbed in the car with my daughter. Can you guess the first thing she asked me?

"What did she give you? Did you get a reward?" she asked expectantly.

"Sure, I got a reward," I told her. "Doing the right thing is the reward. She didn't give me any money and I wouldn't have taken any if she'd offered. I was very happy to do it. It gives me a good feeling to know I'm doing the right thing."

Everyone knows what you have to go through to get a cell phone replaced. It's an ordeal. I'm not saying I'm any sort of saint for doing what I did. That same thing probably happens hundreds of times across the country every day. Still, it's just a small example of how you need to always do the right thing, whether it's in your home life or on the job. Your integrity is always at stake.

GOOD DEEDS ARE THEIR OWN REWARD

I'm sure you've heard the old saying that doing a good deed is its own reward, but do you really believe it? In some cases you're going to get applause and a reward for doing the right thing, but other times you won't even get a pat on the back. Instead, you'll get chewed out or maybe even fired. Hopefully you aren't doing the right thing for the pat on the back because there is no guarantee you're going to get it. Remember, doing the right thing isn't always the same as doing the popular thing. A lot of the time they will coincide, but every once in a while you have to swim upstream to do the right thing. Going against the grain isn't pleasant. You'll get some splinters, but it's worth it in order to keep your integrity intact.

> "Every time I've done something that doesn't feel right, it's ended up not being right."
>
> —*Mario Cuomo*

I knew a guy from Manhattan back when I was just a firefighter. He was a lieutenant when I first met him and he promoted to captain soon afterward. When he made captain, the FDNY sent him to the Bronx.

I'm not sure what your fire department does with promotions, but when you make captain in the FDNY, they make you move. They take you out of your comfort zone, whether it's your regular battalion or division, and they send you to a place where you don't know anybody.

They want to send you someplace that you aren't used to so you can get your legs and learn your new job without being too familiar with everybody. Familiarity can be a good thing, but if team members get too buddy-buddy, little mistakes can happen.

He transferred to the Bronx and landed in a spot on a really good truck. They had plenty of work and all the firefighters were highly motivated, positive members of the team. His first two weeks there, he didn't do anything. A lot of new leaders like to come in and "clean house," making sweeping changes so everyone knows who's in charge.

This captain didn't do that. Instead, he just watched. For two whole weeks he quietly took stock of his team. He learned who filled what role and how good they were at their jobs.

Right off the bat, he noticed that the most senior man in the company was slacking. He had a great reputation. He was the senior man and acted as one of the leaders of the company. Yet the captain saw him coming in late, going home early, practically missing runs, wearing a disheveled uniform. His personal experience was contradicting everything the captain had heard about this guy.

The captain had to ask himself what was going on. Sometimes a guy won't quite live up to his reputation, but in this case it was the polar opposite. There must have been something else going on.

After two weeks of observation, the captain pulled the guy into his office and said, "Look, Billy. I'm the new captain. I know I've only been here a couple of weeks and I don't know you that well, but you're really falling down on the job. I've heard a lot of good things about this firehouse and about you, in particular, but you're just not performing. I'm afraid you may have a drinking problem. I think you need to get some help with that."

The FDNY has a service for psychological and substance abuse help, we always have. Since 9/11, it has grown to a much larger scale, but it's in place for just this type of situation and has been for a long time. Employees of the FDNY can refer themselves to that service for assistance without any negative effects.

The captain said, "It looks to me like you may have a problem and I think you need some help. I'm new here, though, and maybe you've just been having a bad couple of weeks. I'll give you a week to straighten out. If you're good in a week, then I'm fine, too. If not, I'm going to have to refer you. It's a supervisory referral, so it will go on your record. You won't lose your job, but it will stay on your record. Think about that and straighten up if you can." And with that, he dismissed the senior firefighter.

Well, a week went by and the guy was even worse. We spoke earlier about following through, saying what you mean and meaning what you say. Well, in this case the captain was forced to follow through on the referral. He referred the guy to the counseling service unit.

Once that was done, the person referred had to make a phone call and go meet with some people, then they go to "the farm." At the FDNY, we call it "sending a guy to the farm." I'm not sure what really goes on there, but this senior guy was effectively removed from his company.

He was a senior man with the company. He had nearly thirty years on the job and he was gone. How do you think the captain was viewed by the rest of the men in the company after that?

Let's just say he wasn't very popular. There he was, the new guy, and two weeks in he's cutting their oldest and most experienced member. Nobody was being outwardly hostile to the captain, but he wasn't getting a lot of friendly comments around the firehouse, either.

Did he do the right thing?

Yes, absolutely. He absolutely did the right thing. The fact that he didn't get any applause is not only understandable, but acceptable. He did what he had to do. Sometimes part of being a boss, being a leader, is making the unpopular choices. It's part of your job as a leader to do the right thing, even if everybody hates you for it.

A few weeks after the firefighter had been removed from duty, the phone at the firehouse rang. It was the wife of this firefighter; let's call her Mrs. Smith. She asked for the captain. All of the firefighters sitting around thought Mrs. Smith was going to give the captain an earful; really let him have it for giving her husband that supervisory referral. They were mad at him and hoped she had called to tear him a new one.

That wasn't why she had called at all. She called to thank the captain. Mrs. Smith said, "Thank you for taking care of my husband. Thank you for seeing what a lot of people have never taken the time to look at. Thank you for not just putting him to bed or sending him home early, but actually doing something. Everyone else has just swept this under the rug and said, 'He's had thirty years on the job. If he wants to drink a lot, that's fine.' "You probably saved his life," she said. "I'm positive you saved our marriage. He's doing really well now. They're fixing him up. He's going to be back to work in a couple of months and I just wanted to thank you personally."

How's that for a pat on the back and some nice applause?

NO IMMEDIATE VINDICATION

The story John just told had a relatively quick turnaround time. That new captain had a tough few months, but in the grand scheme of things his decision was vindicated in a fairly small amount of time. Ray Hoff, one of our good friends and a retired Chicago battalion chief, told us a story about a time it took a lot longer for him to be vindicated. He had just received a visit from a firefighter. It was a really overwhelming talk, and it was basically the same kind of experience that the new captain had with his senior firefighter. The talk didn't happen two weeks later, however. It took ten years for his pat on the back to come.

This firefighter had just left his office after an hour-long apology. Ray said that he had taken abuse for ten years over this particular firefighter. A decade ago, Ray had referred this firefighter for substance abuse treatment. He had hated Ray ever since, and so had many of the other folks in the firehouse. For ten years, Ray had suffered because he did the right thing. He didn't take the easy way out and let it slide, he forced this guy to get help. Because of that, here this guy was in his office giving him his heartfelt gratitude for over an hour.

He told Ray he'd saved his job and saved his marriage. He said it had taken him a long time to straighten some things out, but he finally realized what Ray had done for him all those years ago. For the longest time he had hated Ray, but in the end he realized Ray was the only one who was really looking out for his best interests. All the other firefighters who were willing to look the other way weren't helping him. The only person who helped him was the man who was willing to make the tough decision, to do the right thing.

The point is that it may take a long time, or you may never get any real applause for doing the right thing, but that shouldn't matter. You should do the right thing *because* it's the right thing, not for any reward or praise.

Sometimes it's not going to be easy. Sometimes it won't be convenient or comfortable. Sometimes it's going to get your butt kicked, but you have to do what's right, anyway.

It may take a long time, or you may never get any real applause for doing the right thing, but that shouldn't matter.

8
INITIATIVE

Do you know what initiative is as it relates to leadership? It's taking the first step. That's exactly what initiative is: to initiate, to start—to begin. There's nothing in there about finishing. There's nothing in there about the size of the job. It has nothing to do with quality. We're just talking about getting the ball rolling.

That's one of the biggest responsibilities of someone in a leadership position in any industry, but it's especially applicable to the fire service. It doesn't have to be at a fire or an emergency situation. You don't need a five-alarm fire to display your leadership skills. As a matter of fact, it's usually the smaller jobs where you'll usually find initiative to be lacking. Nobody wants to get started on committee work, but somebody has to do it. You may have been putting off engine maintenance; cleaning up around the firehouse is never fun. All of those types of things are necessary. Everybody wants to be the leader on the fireground, calling the shots and directing the action, but it takes a real leader to take initiative in the mundane, day-to-day tasks we all have to deal with.

Everybody wants to be the leader on the fireground, calling the shots and directing the action, but it takes a real leader to take initiative in the mundane, day-to-day tasks we all have to deal with.

Somebody has to plan the hundred-year anniversary. Someone needs to organize the softball team. Whatever that task may be, somebody has to take initiative and be a leader. Leadership and initiative are synonymous. Take the World Trade Center, for example (fig 8–1). All sorts of people died that day, both civilians and firefighters. When we think about the folks we know who died that day, we wonder if it took any more initiative to start walking up the steps of that building on that day as it did to walk up the steps of the building that was on fire the day before? Nope. Not one ounce more. Not one ounce more of initiative was required to do that than was required to respond to a fire a week, a month, or a year before that day.

"Don't lose sight of the most important factors that lead to successful leadership: commitment, a passion to make a difference, a vision for achieving positive change, and the courage to take action."

—*Larraine Matusak*

Fig. 8–1. The World Trade Center on September 11, 2001

That was a gigantic event. Everybody knows where they were when that picture was taken, right? It's pretty universal around the country. As when Kennedy was shot or during the moon landing, we all remember where we were on 9/11.

The whole thing lasted just over 100 minutes. Nobody knew, at the moment the snapshot in figure 8–1 was taken, that those two buildings were going to collapse. I didn't know. If you knew, that's wonderful. You're a sharper knife than me—I had no idea.

I talked to lots of people in those 100 minutes. I saw a lot of things, thought about a lot of things. It never occurred to me how that day was going to end. Nobody knew that it was going to be a massive tragedy or that it would take almost three thousand lives.

That's what makes initiative pretty hard sometimes: We don't know how it's going to end. When we go to work, we're not going to the merry-go-round with our kids; we're going into burning buildings. Whether it's the World Trade Center or an ordinary house fire, it takes the same amount of initiative to go into a burning building each time.

Figure 8–2 reminds me of a story regarding FDNY Ladder 15 (fig. 8–2).

Fig. 8–2. One of the World Trade Center towers on September 11, 2001.

Ladder 15 is a truck company in downtown Manhattan, and they were one of the units that responded and operated during the initial stages of the World Trade Center incident. Several months after 9/11, when they released the recordings of the radio transmissions, I listened to them. I heard a lot of interesting and inspiring transmissions on those recordings. I heard my friend, Battalion Chief Orio Palmer, who died that day. He was ascending one of the towers along with several other units. Chief Palmer worked with me preparing members of the FDNY who were studying for upcoming promotional exams. Chief Palmer was in there and he made it up to the seventy-eighth floor of the tower. He made it up to where the planes crashed, and he gave a pretty good report of what was going on up there. This was after it was reported that no one had made it to those floors.

Orio Palmer calls up from the 28th floor and reports a broken stairwell. He calls up from the fifty-ninth floor and reports that he had to climb around some sheetrock. Finally, in these recordings of the radio transmission, you hear someone call him and tell him that there's another plane coming in. There has been a report that there's another plane headed for the building he's in.

What did he say next? Can you take a guess what Orio's instructions were? His instructions were simply, "Keep going." They weren't leaving. They could have said, "Another plane's coming? Let's abandon this building." But they didn't. They kept on going.

Let's talk a little bit about 15 Truck. It's a fairly busy place in lower Manhattan where they run a ton of automatic fire alarms. They respond to a couple thousand runs a year, yet few are working fires. It's not a very active place, not the kind of place that has a waiting list, but those in that company who worked that day—they worked real hard.

Two firefighters in the elevator called "Ladder-One-Five" on the radio and said, "Hey Lou, we're stuck. We're stuck in the elevator. We think it jumped off the tracks or something. We're stuck on the 39th floor."

What were they doing? They were shuttling passengers from the fortieth floor to the lobby. Injured, burned people were being taken there, twenty or thirty at a time. Then they would go right back up and bring down another group.

Now that thing jumps off the track and they're stuck in the elevator. They tell the boss they're stuck. What do they tell him next? They don't say, "Come get us." They don't say, "Mayday!" They said, "Make sure you send those people to another elevator bank. Don't put them in our elevator bank because we're stuck. We'll try to chop our way out." Of course, all those men died up there. All the guys in the elevator died. The lieutenant died.

Orio Palmer died. But the lesson we should learn from their actions is their determination and their initiative.

Those people were just doing their jobs. None of them knew how that day was going to end. None of them knew those buildings were going to fall down. That was just the biggest operation they'd ever had.

TAKE INITIATIVE ALL THE TIME

We've been to dozens of "biggest operation ever" incidents. They only happen one at a time, but when you're there, you think that's the biggest job you've been to. As you're watching it unfold, you're thinking, "This is the biggest one I've ever seen!" However, you can't just take initiative on the big calls. You have to practice it every day.

Sometimes, in the job we do, there's a doubt. You ask yourself, "Am I really doing the right thing?" When they send firefighters in to a burning building, nearly all officers ask themselves if they're making the right call. "Maybe we shouldn't be attacking. Maybe we should be retreating and taking up a defensive posture."

> "Progress always involves risk; you can't steal second base and keep your foot on first."
>
> —*Frederick Wilcox*

We're always worried about how an incident is going to turn out. Is it going to be positive or negative? Sometimes you have to put those thoughts out of your mind. Effective leaders have to be able to ignore that doubt and do what they think is best. That goes for all types of operational leadership, not just in the firehouse. If you can't have faith in your choices, nobody following you is going to have faith either.

If you can't have faith in your choices, nobody following you is going to have faith either.

That type of initiative transfers over to other areas, too. How you act at a softball game, or when you're just at the firehouse hanging out, is how you're going to act on the fireground. If you don't take initiative around the firehouse, keeping the place clean and neat, then how can you be expected to take initiative when you're at an incident?

You don't go into the World Trade Center every day to save thousands of lives, but you do hang out in the firehouse on most days. You may think they're different, but it takes the same type of initiative to respond to a one-story house fire in your neighborhood as it does to take that first step up the stairwell of the World Trade Center (fig. 8–3).

Fig. 8–3. House fire in Norman, Oklahoma

The point we're trying to get across is this: It's easy to show initiative when the bell goes off. As a good leader you need to show initiative the rest of the time too. When it's time to take care of your apparatus, do maintenance on your tools, perform a fire inspection, or just do your daily drill, show your initiative by doing them all as well as you can. The challenge is getting your folks to show that same kind of initiative when running on that same false alarm (figs. 8–4 and 8–5). We've had tragedy strike before on that "same old false alarm." The idea is to never get caught by surprise. Always try to stay a step ahead by being prepared and thinking ahead.

Figs. 8–4 and 8–5. Crew from FDNY Engine 45 in the Bronx ready to go to work at the "false alarm" the same as they would be at a working fire: every time!

We've said it many times before: "Why do we have to wait for a good fire for us all to get along?" The answer is simple: it's harder. It's more of a challenge for you as a leader to display initiative when the bell's not going off. Getting people to follow you around the firehouse, like that tower ladder lieutenant, the "working officer," takes something special. When people gravitate to you all the time, not just at a fire, then you know you're a true leader.

It's easier when the bell goes off, but still challenging enough. The question is, how good are you at getting people to do the *other* things they need to do when the bell's not going off?

9
INNOVATION

Innovation is a big part of the fire service. In our profession, innovation saves lives. There are several different types of innovation. Sometimes you innovate with new leadership skills, sometimes you innovate with new tactics, other times, it can be something as simple as trying out a more effective tool.

There was a time when the FDNY couldn't buy new tools. Whatever you had better work. If it broke, you had to fix it yourself. Firefighters would go down to the local hardware store and buy a new axe handle, and then try to attach it themselves. That's a pretty simple example of effective innovation. Tools were broken and the department wasn't going to fix them, so they had to figure out a way to make it work on their own.

Sometimes you have to innovate on how you deal with folks in the firehouse. When we talked about the "working lieutenant," that was an example of innovation in the supervisory role. You don't have to treat every infraction the same way. Some people respond to simple requests and others need a firmer hand. Learning which is which, and being able to deal with both types, is a true mark of leadership.

Some people respond to simple requests and others need a firmer hand. Learning which is which, and being able to deal with both types, is a true mark of leadership.

If you act like a robot and treat every person the same, regardless of their situation, and regardless of their contributions, then you might as well have a clerk running your firehouse. Let's say you have a new rule in your firehouse: If you come in late, you will lose an hour's pay. As soon as you implement that rule, two firefighters come in late. The first one has never been late for a shift in thirty years. He's always there thirty minutes early, and he always has been. He said he had an emergency at home and it would never happen again. The other one has been late nearly every day for thirty years. If you're willing to treat both of those situations the same and hand out equal punishment, then you might as well have a clerk running your firehouse. There's no need for officers. We don't need opinions. We don't need to interface with the rank and file. We don't need to decipher or decide or any of that. We just need a clerk who dictates policy from a "book of rules." Why are we paying all these officers when we could just have a $13,000/year clerk tell us what to do?

The reason we don't do that is innovation. We're constantly looking for ways to get better, improve survivability, and lower property damages. Each new situation that arises may require innovation.

Take a look at figure 9–1. It shows a three-story frame building on fire. This is a really good job going. Strong smoke is showing from the A side, and it looks like the vent crew is on the roof. There are a couple of aerial ladders up. There's an engine off to the left side of the building. We have all sorts of tactical operations going on in that picture.

This fire was handled by the A shift at Station 2. Twenty-four hours later, the "B" shift responds to a fire in an identical building. The fire starts in the same area and extends the same way as the first fire the day before. Do you think the rigs would be parked exactly the same way the second time? Would the ladder be put up in the same spot by the second crew? Would the ventilation hole be cut in exactly the same place? Would the second line be brought into the building by the same company? Probably not.

A lot of things might be different. People might be using different tactics. Someone might prefer a different tool for ventilation and so the team uses a circular saw instead of a chainsaw. The strategy of putting the fire out and controlling the loss might be the same, but the crew on day two will probably handle the fire differently from the crew on the day before.

Fig. 9–1. Each situation that arises may require innovation.

"A person who never made a mistake never tried anything new."

—*Albert Einstein*

Why would all these things be different? Because we all innovate based on our experience and training. We've said it before several times, but everyone is unique. Everyone has a unique set of experiences. Everyone has been to a different set of training sessions and exposed to different ideas.

You could have two people come out of the training academy, then go to the same engine, work the same shift for ten years together, never miss a day, work every single fire together, and ten years later, they're going to be different firefighters. They're going to have different ideas on how to get things done, because everyone has a different perspective on things. Those two firefighters will probably have a lot of similarities, but their personal perspectives won't be identical, so they'll take different lessons from their experiences, even if they're virtually identical.

DON'T BE A ROBOT

We see it all the time: businesses fail because they get too machine-like in the way they do business. They stop treating customers like people and instead treat them like numbers. As soon as that starts to happen, once innovation stops and stagnation starts, then the writing is on the wall. The same thing goes for fire chiefs. I'm sure most everyone has had an experience with a chief or a superior officer who runs the battalion like a machine. What ends up happening in that situation? You get a bunch of clock watchers. You know the type, every job has them. These become the workers who are out the door the second their shift is over. The best job in the world becomes more of a task than a profession or career. It sucks all the joy out of being a firefighter.

Figure 9–2 is a picture that was taken some time during the first week after 9/11. You can see in the background where the walls are still standing. The smoke is still rising from the collapse zone. If you look right behind us, you can see something that looks like huge strands of hair. That "hair" was simply part of the miles and miles of cable that was stretched all over the place when the buildings fell.

I didn't get that picture until about a year later. Somebody sent it to me. I can't remember exactly where or when it was taken, but I remember every last thing we did there, and there was nothing normal about it. Everything we did in the first weeks and months after 9/11 was brand new, it wasn't like anything we'd ever done before.

We put on the same shirt, but outside of that everything changed. Everything was innovation. Everything from the way we transported tools to the way we cut steel changed that day. We had to innovate on the fly and come up with new techniques for everything, because none of us had ever been through anything like that before; we didn't have procedures for this.

Fig. 9–2. Ground Zero less than a week after the attacks

You need to be prepared, because even though something the size and scope of 9/11 probably isn't going to happen to you, there's a chance that something big and bad, unique, and catastrophic will strike your town. If it does, you have to be ready to innovate.

Some people are very structured and unable to think outside the box. I'm not a big "outside the box" type of guy. If you ask some of the people I work with, they'll tell you I'm a structured guy, so obviously I'm not telling you to cut out structure. Structure is important.

However, when something happens that is out of the ordinary, you have to be prepared to react. Pick up a different tool, use a different signal, assign some different people, whatever the situation warrants.

THE BULL'S EYE

Have you ever been through something unique, gigantic, dangerous, and extreme, where you were forced to do something you wouldn't normally do? If so, then you understand what we're saying. It can be difficult, but you have to plan for the unexpected so you'll be at least somewhat prepared.

Failure to hit the bull's eye is never the fault of the target. If every arrow you shoot hits down at seven o'clock, then aim up and slightly to the right (fig. 9–3). If you're not hitting the bull's eye, then you have to recognize it and make improvements.

Fig. 9–3. Failure to hit the bull's eye is never the fault of the target. To improve your aim, improve yourself.

That's a major flaw that we see in a lot of successful people: the inability to adapt. That's why they reach a certain level and top out, never seeming to be able to get any higher. Hopefully neither one of our wives read this, because we're here to tell you that nobody's perfect. Everyone has flaws. The key is to recognize your flaws and work around them.

Wherever you're lacking, whether it's operational, tactical, or just with your people skills, you have to see where that flaw is and work to improve it. Maybe you don't run drills that well. Maybe you just don't talk to your subordinates that well. Whatever leadership component you need to work on, you should strive to always be improving yourself. You won't ever improve your aim if you don't practice. The same applies to your leadership.

Wherever you're lacking, whether it's operational, tactical, or just with your people skills, you have to see where that flaw is and work to improve it.

Not everyone has the ability of self-improvement. A lot of firefighters get promoted and then become scared of showing any weakness, never realizing that it's okay not to know everything. That you might make a mistake once in a while and have to change gears or direction.

It's like when I was younger and in school and played baseball. When I had a few bad at-bats, I'd look at the bat like there was something wrong with it, and blame it. Coach Burson would say, "Rick, it's not the bat. It's your swing, buddy."

Unfortunately, some instructors do the exact same thing. Their students just outright fail, and rather than think they might be to blame, they blame the students. Others will immediately assume they've done something wrong.

"How did I drop the ball that much?" you'll ask yourself. You beat yourself up for a while, then you try to figure out what went wrong.

There are two possibilities. Either the instructor did a poor job, maybe missed something: the curriculum was not right, the objectives weren't clear or appropriate, or something didn't work on the instructional side of things. Or there is something wrong with the students. Problems with students usually fall into two categories. Either they have an attitude problem and they didn't give it their all, or they might have a learning disability.

Back when I was a young officer, I had a driver on my crew. This guy was forty-four years old. He was tough and could pump his tail off, and when he was inside, he would never leave your side. When we would have an exam, this great firefighter would never pass the written section. We went over it and I helped him study, but when he went to retake the test, he failed again and would laugh about it.

Needless to say I got upset. I asked him, "What's wrong with you? We studied a lot. How could you fail that test? This all reflects on me, too. I'm your officer, the one that's responsible for your success. I don't know what to do, Jack. I'm done."

After I went off on the guy, I stopped and looked at him and he was crying. He looked up at me through his tears and said, "Rick, I can't read."

That was one of the times in my life where I just wanted to dig a hole and jump in. I felt horrible. I was so wrapped up in myself and all the work I'd done to prepare this guy that I didn't see his problem. I thought, "I did everything I was supposed to. How could you let me down like this?" That was the first time that I realized my people skills might not be as sharp as I thought. The truth of the matter was, he didn't let me down, I let him down. I was so busy being a smartass young know-it-all officer that I misread the whole thing. I missed an incredible opportunity to help someone and be a good mentor. You know, the kind of officer you can depend on, especially when things are not going right.

At that point I had to make a major adjustment. I went to this guy and sat down to talk it out. I had to be more sensitive than usual. I wanted to figure out a way to help him. I went to the boss and said, "We've got a little situation here. I'd like to give Jack oral exams instead of written ones."

I explained what was going on and the boss gave me the okay. Sure enough, Jack passed all the oral exams with flying colors. He was a great firefighter; he just had never learned how to read. We even got him enrolled in a reading program.

I'm not sure how it ended up because I moved on in my career, but I know I had to adjust my aim that day. I was focused too much on myself and I failed to see the target. I failed because I didn't recognize the fact that he had a learning disability.

One of my favorite sayings about firefighters is, "We're good at reading smoke, we're not the best at reading people." In that case, I was awful at reading a person. Once I adjusted my outlook, everyone was able to move forward in a positive and constructive manner.

ARE YOU AN INNOVATOR?

Let's say you're a fire instructor with a class of twenty students. If, at the end of your class, twelve of those twenty students fail the test, then who is at fault? You are! Surely, you, the instructor would say, "That can't be right. Those failures were all from the worst part of the company and that's why they don't get it."

Wrong. If you're an instructor and half your class fails, then you're not doing it well. You have to do something different. You need to change your tactics, change your terminology, change your approach, and change whatever you have to change in order to reach them. It doesn't matter if you're a chief, an instructor, a mom or dad, a CEO, or the leader of a scout troop. If the people under you aren't getting it, aren't showing improvement, aren't excelling, then you have to prove yourself.

What kind of innovator are you? How can you change your tactics to get a different result? How good are your problem solving skills?

It helps to think like a paramedic. Most firefighters do some level of EMS these days, so you should know what we're talking about. When you take emergency medical courses, they teach you to treat the underlying cause. You don't just open up the drug box and start throwing meds at somebody. Are you open-minded enough to look past the symptoms you're seeing in the firehouse and find the cause of the problems you're facing?

Most of the time, if someone isn't doing what you want them to, you'll find out there's a good reason. If a firefighter is coming in late or underperforming, then you'll have to sit him or her down and have "the talk." We've found that you usually discover there's something else going on. It may be problems at home. There could be issues with finances. Whatever it is that's affecting their work, you need to find that out.

You can't just say, "You're late all the time and you're out. Boom! You're done." You have to see the bigger picture.

If you give that response every time, you haven't really solved anything, have you? You've just handed out discipline. You haven't fixed the problem or come up with any solutions. As the leader, that's your job. We are expected to protect people's careers, not end them. If you just want to send people packing, that's your prerogative; however, we believe it makes you a poor leader. It's your job, as a leader, to try to help whenever you can.

We are expected to protect people's careers, not end them.

You won't have all the answers. People who think they have all the answers never do. Some people think all the answers they'll ever need are in their heads, their offices, or their desk drawers. That's not true for anybody. There is always more to learn. There is always more to learn and there is always someone out there who knows or understands something that you are having trouble with.

Every person who reads this book will have unique experiences. Those experiences might be something that someone else can learn from. It's always better to learn from somebody else's mistake than to make it yourself. We both coach and train firefighters who are studying for promotion, whether for a captain's test or a battalion chief's test. We tell those aspiring officers all the time that once they're promoted, they're going to be the "new guys." Lots of departments "bounce" or rotate their new officers around. The FDNY likes to send new officers to an area they aren't familiar with. Many other departments do the same.

As a newly promoted officer, you'll be the one bouncing around. You'll be going to places you've never been in your entire life, and you probably won't go back to once you transfer out. You act as sort of a substitute teacher, stepping into somebody else's firehouse for a short period. What's great about this process is that it places the new officers into an area or environment they don't know or have a history with the firefighters they will be supervising. This usually makes it easier for these new officers to apply their supervisory skills.

It's not advisable to jump right in and start making changes. People will resist them, and they will automatically dislike whoever is doing it. Also, you probably won't be the only officer involved. It's inadvisable for you to just come in and make changes without talking to them first.

Even if it's your first night in your new firehouse, if you see a problem then you need to solve it. What would be your first step? Where would you go to get the answer?

One thing to consider is to ask the most senior person in the company. You may be the higher ranking officer, but if there's a firefighter who has been there for twelve years, you need to seek his or her advice. If there isn't another officer around to ask, pick up the phone and call somebody. Call a friend. Call a mentor. Just call the guy who was your lieutenant when you were a firefighter. Call someone who has been there before and ask how he or she would handle the situation.

I have a long list of experienced mentors and friends I can call. After thirty-three years in the fire department, I've built up quite a Rolodex. I'm still willing to use that list and ask for advice when I'm not sure what to do.

I've got a buddy, a captain who retired to Florida, and I call him every once in a while. I'll ask, "I've got this really weird situation. What do you think about this?"

I throw different problems at him and he's usually got some really useful answers. We were firefighters together years ago and have remained friends ever since. We talk often about the fire department and how things are going. We both bring problems and difficult situations to each other for another perspective. Even though we have not worked together in years, our accumulated experiences can be used to tackle just about any problem.

Everybody should be part of a network. It's not something you really have to work at, either. It's just something you naturally grow as you've gone through your career as a firefighter. Look back on your history. Think of the people you're closest to, or maybe even people you're not that close with, but that you know are still on the job. Most anybody in the fire service is going to be willing to help out a brother in need.

Every day, the FDNY puts out a "chief sheet." It lists all the battalion and deputy chiefs working that day on both the day tour and the night tour.

I look at that sheet every day I work to see which chiefs I know who are working. Other officers can see my name on their sheet, and they know where to find me if they need to. I occasionally get calls from people I haven't seen in a while.

This reminds me of a story I heard about a battalion chief in a department somewhere in New Jersey. This chief contacts a friend of his, who is also a battalion chief with a little more experience than him, and tells him the following story:

He was working a night tour in a battalion that he was not very familiar with and he made a routine visit to one of the engine companies one evening at around 9:30 p.m. He knocked on the front door and was waiting for a firefighter to let him in. He knocked several more times and nobody answered the door. Finally, a young firefighter could be seen dashing down the apparatus floor toward the front door. When the firefighter looked out the window and saw the chief, he quickly turned and ran back toward the rear of the apparatus floor. The chief couldn't believe what just happened, and he began to knock again. A minute or so later, a gray-haired lieutenant arrived at the door and swung it open and said hello to the chief. "What can we do for you chief?" the lieutenant asked, while holding open the door. The chief told him he was just stopping by for a quick visit to see how everything is going. The lieutenant told the chief, "It's really not a good time for a visit, Chief." The chief, not really expecting such a response, wasn't quite sure what to do, but just as quickly, decided to take the lieutenant's advice and stop by some other time.

Later, the chief asked his friend about what he thought regarding his decision to skip the visit. The more senior chief told him that he would have done the same thing. "Boy, I'm glad to hear you say that, and I'm glad this is over," he said. His friend told him it was not over, and although he decided not to make the visit, he still needed to find out why it wasn't such a good time for the visit. Additionally, he told him that he would probably hear from the lieutenant sometime that evening or the next morning, and the lieutenant would almost certainly explain what occurred.

The following morning, the chief called his friend back again and told him that he had just returned to quarters from a visit over at the suspect engine company. The lieutenant invited him over to explain what had happened. It turned out that an off-duty member had entered the engine quarters about thirty minutes prior to the chief's visit, and he had been drinking. Not heavily, but he had been out with another firefighter and their wives for dinner and drinks. They dropped him off at the firehouse where he was going to stay the night and go on duty the following morning, saving him a long commute. Unfortunately, he ran into another firefighter who he does not get along with very well, and a small fight ensued. Both firefighters were banged up a bit, and the television was knocked off its shelf, basically exploding. Just as this circus was happening, the chief arrived and knocked on the door. The lieutenant explained that there was no way he could allow the chief to enter and get involved in this situation. This was a great company, with a great reputation, and he wanted to protect that. He also told the chief he had handled the discipline for both members, and that they were both also paying for a new television for the company. The chief accepted the lieutenant's explanation and also suggested he try to prevent these types of events rather than handle them afterward.

PATIENCE IS A VIRTUE

Trust is a big element in that entire story. First off, the chief had to have faith in his friend's advice. If he hadn't made that phone call, he might have jumped right back into his car and forced his way into the situation. Trust is what he also showed in this lieutenant. He has to trust in the lieutenant's leadership skills, his decision making, and his conflict resolution abilities in this case. Sometimes trusting your officers may come back to bite you, but usually they prove they're worthy of your trust.

There are still some officers reading this and saying, "I don't care what Lasky and Salka say, I would have gone back over there!" That's fine. We're not telling you how to run your department. All we're saying is that you need to think about the consequences of your actions, both good and bad. Had this chief forced his way into that situation, not only would he have created more work for himself, but he would also be effectively telling that lieutenant, "I don't trust your judgment, I'll handle this."

That was a problem that solved itself. The chief didn't need to do a thing about it. We're also not saying that you need to look the other way and hope major issues sort themselves out. You don't want to walk around with your eyes closed, but you need to trust your officers enough that if one of them says to you, "Now isn't a good time, Chief," you can leave and have faith that they're handling the situation properly.

There have been numerous occasions where we have each walked into a firehouse kitchen to have a cup of coffee and visit with the troops, and have walked right into the middle of a "conversation." Many times, the best choice of action was to turn around and walk out or to another room and give them a chance to work it through. Again, if you jump into the middle of every issue, every conflict, every counseling session, you'll never give your company officers a chance to hone their skills when it comes to conflict resolution. They'll look to you each and every time they need to make a decision or possibly just get frustrated with you getting involved each time and say, "Why do I bother? He's just going to come in and take over anyway." Give them a chance. With a little bit of ahead-of-time guidance, you almost always see better results.

If you jump into the middle of every issue, every conflict, every counseling session, you'll never give your company officers a chance to hone their skills when it comes to conflict resolution.

You'll find that a little patience will save you a lot of hassle. As we get older we've realized that if you just wait a little bit, things will sort themselves out. You don't have to ignore problems, just give them a day. Personal issues like those this chief was dealing with often sort themselves out and you can go on about your business.

If you don't blow up, it's usually to your benefit. Don't just burst in and start grilling the troops. Take some time and read your people. Sometimes we're so used to reacting to emergencies that we rush in as fast as possible to get the job done quickly and treat all situations with the same eagerness.

YOU WILL BE TESTED

We hear all the time from officers who think their members are only doing things to see how they react. It doesn't matter what part of the country they're from, it's the same circus with different clowns. We've been there. When you first get promoted and go to that new firehouse, you may not know it, but you're going to be tested. The troops will be asking questions, doing little things to test the boundaries, see who you are and how you measure up.

When a new officer works a shift, or maybe a short assignment of a week or two, the firefighters will really start to inquire about his or her history. The first thing they'll want to know is where you came from. They know you're a lieutenant, but they want to know where you were a firefighter. It's not just firefighters, but in many professions the new people are going to have stuff thrown at them to see how they handle it. Furthermore, when an officer has a short tour, maybe just a week or two, they will really try to "unbutton" him.

A young firefighter comes into your office and says, "Hey, Lou. Can I take a flyer?" That means, "Can I have 45 minutes to run an errand?" He continues, "I've got my kid's car with me. He blew a tire yesterday and it's got the donut spare on right now. The tire store is a mile from here, so I brought the car with me. Do you mind if I take a quick trip down there to get a new tire?"

What would be your answer? Would you let him go? That takes you from four people down to three. Would you tell him no? You might tell him you're busy right now and you'll come find him in a minute to talk about it. That's a great way to buy yourself some time to reason out your response and think about this decision. You can even take that time to pick up the phone and call someone in your network for advice.

A lot of that will depend on your own experience. There's no tried and true answer for every situation. You have to figure out the best path as you go. You would have to ask yourself if this is a trustworthy firefighter, a punctual firefighter. If he is, then you might let him slip out for fifteen minutes to take care of the flat tire. If he's less reliable, then you might have to tell him no. Another option might be to tell him to throw the tire onto the apparatus, and that they can stop by the tire store when returning from the next alarm response.

If you let him go and then you get called out on a run and the chief sees you, you're going to have to explain why you only have three people on your rig. You're not going to be able to lie. You just have to tell the chief what decision you made and why. There's no right answer. Either way you're going to be taking a little bit of a risk. You could take the safe path and always say no, but eventually your people will resent you for being rigid and inflexible.

IT ALL COMES BACK TO INNOVATION

Of course, the main theme is innovation. Sometimes you're going to have to improvise and make do. You won't always have the luxury of a full team, the newest tools, or the biggest department. When that happens, there are other options. There are ways around difficult issues that can still make it work. No matter what the situation is, just take a few minutes and think it through.

> "A wise man changes his mind;
> a fool never does."
>
> —*Spanish proverb*

We kill firefighters and we regret the decisions we made based on the flurry of emotions during the height of an incident. If you make decisions based on emotions, people may die. If you make decisions based on common sense, you vastly improve the chances of survival for your entire company. An innovative lieutenant might see the flat tire problem and say, "Hop in the car and we'll follow you on the rig. Drop it off, jump back on the rig, and we're back in service!"

That way you don't have to endanger the rest of your company so that this firefighter can run an errand, but you don't have to look like a rigid officer who doesn't look out for his or her people. All we're saying is that you have to have a little bit of flexibility. You have to be able to deal with different situations when they arise. A lot of times, there won't be an obvious "right" answer. Sometimes you just need to flex a little bit to see the big picture. There are a lot of variables. Who is involved? When did it happen? How long did this go on?

★★★★★★★★

If you make decisions based on emotions, people may die. If you make decisions based on common sense, you vastly improve the chances of survival for your entire company.

★★★★★★★★

Sometimes you may make a decision to bend the rules a little bit. Unfortunately, if you get caught, you'll have to deal with the consequences. Let's say you decided to let the firefighter go get the tire fixed and the errand took half an hour. During that time, you go out on a call and the chief finds out. You can't pass on that responsibility. You can't say, "Well, I called Lieutenant so-and-so and got an okay to let him go." When you're the leader, the buck stops with you. That's why you should always take some time to think about your decisions. If you have to back them up to a superior, you want to at least be able to explain why you made the choices you did.

10
INSIGHT

One of the more overlooked elements of leadership is insight. A great leader must have quality insight into his organization. What does it mean to have insight into your organization? What do you have to know about your department in order to be considered "insightful"? You might be looking for some big cosmic answer, but it's actually some pretty basic stuff. You have to know what your organization is about. You have to know the job you're expected to do inside and out, top to bottom. You have to understand the smaller tasks that make up the larger job. You have to anticipate the barriers you could face. All in all, you need to understand the mission of your organization, from the smallest detail to the largest incident. You need a crystal ball!

All in all, you need to understand the mission of your organization, from the smallest detail to the largest incident.

What is insight all about? Where does it come from? It's not the equipment. Everybody doesn't use the same kind of nozzle, much less the same apparatus. Is your apparatus even red? Many aren't these days. If you're one of the unlucky ones riding around on a yellow rig, don't worry. It just hasn't ripened yet. Leave it out in the sun for a while. We're just kidding. A fire engine is a fire engine, just take ownership of it and take care of it no matter what color it is.

There is usually a reason that a town moves away from the red fire apparatus. Some go to white because they reflect sunlight and keep firefighters cooler. Others go to yellow or lime green because they have higher visibility. Whatever the reason is, if your department is using a different colored rig, you'd better know why. We can promise you that some young firefighter is going to approach you and ask you why your rigs are yellow when everybody else drives red ones. Even if there is no known reason, it would be nice to know that so you can answer intelligently.

IT'S THE LITTLE THINGS

You need to be aware of all the little details. Why is your badge the shape it is? Why do you have an eagle or a bear on it? All these little details can help to provide insight into the organization and teach younger firefighters why we do what we do. This story never gets old: We were at the FDIC about ten years ago and were shocked by two younger firefighters sitting next to us. A man dressed up as Ben Franklin came out to give a speech—Benjamin Franklin, who we should know as one of the founding fathers of the United States (fig. 10–1). Not only that, but he's widely credited as being the founder of America's first fire service. When the Franklin re-enactor came out, these two firefighters sitting next to us turned to each other and asked, "What's with the old guy?"

> "A leader has the vision and conviction that a dream can be achieved. He inspires the power and energy to get it done."
>
> —*Ralph Lauren*

Fig. 10–1. Benjamin Franklin, a founding father, created America's first fire company.

We travel the country all the time and ask people questions about their departments. It can be discouraging sometimes when they can't give good answers. We ask about their department, how it started, when or where it was founded, or why they do what they do. So many firefighters we meet can't answer those simple questions. We're not saying you have to become a historian of all your department's little known facts. We both have friends who are heavily involved in collecting historical fire memorabilia. You know the type, those with leather buckets and brass speaking trumpets from the 1800s in their living room? That's fine, but we're not suggesting you have to become the department's historian. Just be sure you know all of the most important facts.

You should at least have a basic understanding of the history of your organization. Did it start in 1868 or 1968? It's not only important for you to have this information, but you have to be able to pass it on to the next generation.

Remember Captain Jason Frei from the Marine Corps? He said some great things about the corps. When he was asked about some of the more amazing things he'd seen, he talked about an 18-year-old driver who was willing to die for a captain he met that morning because he knew what it meant to be a marine. That kid knew the history of the Marine Corps. He knew why the uniform was that color. He knew what the Marine Corps emblem meant. He knew the value of his organization, and there was a reason he knew it so well.

The Marine Corps doesn't get kids like that by accident; they instill their values in all those young kids from day one. When they get to basic training, from whatever town they grew up in, they're taught about all the great marines who came before them (fig. 10–2). They're taught about the great sacrifices made and battles won by their predecessors. They're taught about all the great things that marines have accomplished, so that when they put on their uniforms, they feel that they are a part of something greater than themselves.

Fig. 10–2. USMC Marine Brian Salka (third from left) in basic training

That's why people risk their lives in battle. It's not because they really get along with some captain they just met that morning. It's because they're all marines and they have a code to live up to. We can have that same impact on the people who work for us. The fire department has a rich history and tradition. If you will just pass on some insight into that tradition to the younger members in your department, you'll go a long way toward strengthening your entire organization for the future.

If you will just pass on some insight into that tradition to the younger members in your department, you'll go a long way toward strengthening your entire organization for the future.

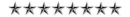

There are a lot of firefighters out there learning about the FDNY from guys in my generation. I'm teaching guys who weren't even born yet when I started out on the job!

I tell them all about Vinny Dunn and Smokey Joe Martin. I tell them about all the great fires. I talk about the Waldbaum's fire in 1978 where six firefighters died. I talk about working with a guy who fell through the ceiling with all those men. I remember listening to him tell the story about falling through the roof and being trapped between the two roofs with the other firefighters, and lots of heat and smoke and fire. A lot of those other men didn't survive that day, but he did. He saw a hole and dove right through it, falling onto the supermarket floor below.

When I tell that story to the kids in my firehouse, they listen intently. That's what having insight into your organization is all about. You're passing on the values of your organization. You're teaching them about the impact your department has had on your community so these younger firefighters are aware of the weight they're carrying around with them on the rig. You're teaching them about the sacrifices that firefighters are sometimes forced to make. You're teaching them about what is expected of them by the job and by their fellow firefighters.

You have to let them know they aren't just kids with yellow hats; they are a part of the fire department. Their integrity reflects on the department as a whole. Their honorable service will ensure that people continue to respect and revere the fire department.

There's no doubt in my mind that if we don't continue to pass on our traditions and mission, they *will* go away. Everyone needs to be aware that the uniforms we wear and the medals we pin on our chests or collars aren't about individual accomplishments. There may be some individual act that a medal represents, but what the uniform and medals really stand for is an entire heritage.

How can you understand the mission of your organization if you don't understand its history? How can you really believe in the fire service if you can't grasp its mission?

The answer is simple: you can't.

LEARN FROM THE PAST

Our shared heritage is a unique aspect to the fire service. We don't all use the same tactics. Our policies and procedures vary widely. We don't even all stretch hose the same way. The one thing we share is heritage. It's a big deal for younger firefighters when a seasoned veteran will sit down and share details about the history of the fire service with them. They love to hear about the old days. Not only that, they need to learn from our mistakes.

If we aren't sharing history with the younger troops, we're only damning them to repeat our mistakes. Along with respect for our traditions, we have to instill in them a healthy knowledge of our shortcomings. We're so worried about our stock portfolios or our new pickup trucks that we aren't doing what we should to pass on the heritage of the fire department to the people who are its future. We're not passing on information, yet we all wonder why LODD numbers aren't going down? Enough with the school of hard knocks.

If we aren't sharing history with the younger troops, we're only damning them to repeat our mistakes.

When we were both coming up in our departments, the bosses we really loved working under were the officers who provided the most insight into the job. They had the most information about the policies of the department and they knew its history, too. They knew the history not only of the department, but even of a particular battalion or company.

At this point many people reading this are going to say, "I have too much on my plate already. I'm trying to run an understaffed department on a shoe-string budget. Where am I supposed to find the time to become a history professor, too?" We're not suggesting you have to know every little detail. You just need to grasp the important stuff. The firefighters who have a good understanding of where a department came from are the ones who will make a difference in where that department goes.

Core values serve as the foundation for everything we're discussing in this book.

I had a beautiful place in Lewisville. God, I loved it. It's not a huge town, but they've got a pretty busy fire department. The city has about seven hundred employees, give or take.

Lewisville had nine values, as a city. Over the years I asked every city department director, and, with the exception of a couple, very few could list all nine. Good intentions, great words to live by, a great city with great bosses, but we were just missing our mark a little bit.

As a fire department, we had three core values: pride, honor, and integrity. Those three things served as the foundation for everything we did.

Along with pride, I naturally include ownership. If you take ownership of the rig or the firehouse, then you're going to take pride in its appearance. If you're working a shift, that's *your* shift or rig, and that's *your* firehouse. That's why you take care of them.

Too many firefighters are just doing things because the chief said they should. They clean the rig because that's what their department does on Tuesdays. They don't take any ownership of the firehouse, so how can they show pride in it?

I want to see a firefighter who says, "You don't have to tell me, Chief. That's *my* rig. I'm sorry it's dirty. I'll get on the guys and we'll get this taken care of." That's a person who has taken ownership of the engine.

When we're able to instill ownership in firefighters, then we've done our jobs as leaders. When your firefighters say, "That's my tool today. That's my rig. That's my station," you can feel confident that you've given them the ability to claim the job for their own.

OWN THE FIREHOUSE

The FDNY conducts annual inspections every year. Many departments have the same type of exercise. Once a year every single firehouse, every single apparatus, every single company office is inspected. A schedule is issued that sets the date the inspection will be held in each of the firehouses. This schedule comes out many weeks ahead of the inspection date to give the companies sufficient time to get every area, tool, and apparatus into shape.

You'd be amazed how much junk can accumulate in a single year. The sidewalk is full of old washing machines, hangers, garbage from emptied lockers, whatever you can think of. Tons of stuff gets thrown away. Once all the old garbage has been cleaned out, the entire place is cleaned from top to bottom. All the windows are washed. All the floors are waxed. All the desks get polished. All the lines on the apparatus floor are repainted. Every single thing in the firehouse is redone.

During inspection, everyone has to show up. The deputy chief arrives for roll call, then he walks through the whole firehouse, including the company office. He goes through the files and checks the last building inspection to make sure it was done properly. He discusses notes from the record book with the lieutenant. He inspects the apparatus, and he even inspects every engine compartment.

The inspection can last several hours, and is repeated every year. That means that every single year the firehouse is cleaned, buffed, and repainted. Thank God for annual inspections, or every firehouse in the FDNY would be over the rafters with junk. It's hard to imagine what they would be like if stuff was allowed to build up more than thirty years in a place like that. An important thing that may get missed in all that work is the aspect of ownership. When members have to clean and care for their firehouse, it helps instill in them a sense of ownership.

Some of the younger firefighters you're going to deal with don't understand the concept of ownership because they've had everything done for them. Mom or Dad always kept the house clean and made the car payments. They never felt real ownership for anything growing up.

It's up to you as the company officer to sit them down and explain what you expect. That's the only way they're going to grow into the type of fire-fighters you want in your department. So many officers get mad when their firefighters aren't doing things exactly the way they want them to, but since they've never explained exactly what that way is, they have no one to blame but themselves.

It's up to you as the company officer to sit them down and explain what you expect.

Teaching the younger generation is also the only way you will get to the point where you can properly delegate. If you can't trust them with the department tools, how are you going to trust them to make life-or-death decisions on the fireground? However, once you've built them up to the point where you can trust their decisions, they become highly valuable members of the team.

If you can't trust them with the department tools, how are you going to trust them to make life-or-death decisions on the fireground?

Some of our greatest, smartest, and most talented young people are being minimized and ignored. So many places we see the "problem solver" has to be the person wearing the collar pins. People don't listen to ideas from the lower levels (fig. 10–3). Firefighters have a lot of good ideas on how to improve the fire service, but they're never given a chance by the brass.

Fig. 10–3. Officers aren't the only ones with good ideas. Listen to your people!

Simply listening to people is a good way to empower them. You can develop a level of trust with your team if you just lend them your ear every once in a while. Once that trust is built up, you can use it to your advantage. Empowering your people is a two-way street. Once you've placed a level of responsibility on your firefighters, you can demand results. You need to hold them accountable.

It's a great thing when your firefighters feel responsible to you, but you can't abuse that gift. You have to accept someone's best efforts. We've both seen some very bad management methods that drive people into the ground. The idea is that your people will always strive to improve if you never praise their efforts. Unfortunately, that only works up to a point. Eventually, if you don't learn to accept your firefighters' best efforts, they will give up and never rise to the next level. Sometimes they just won't do anything right. Sometimes they aren't working hard and you have to get on them. Other times, you need to sit them down and coach them in the right direction.

We're big fans of constructive criticism. When someone comes to you and asks for feedback, first point out where their work is up to standards, then add a pointer or two about improvement. "You know, that looks good. Can you do me a favor and just add this little bit here?" You have to instill your troops with confidence. Once they have confidence, the quality of their work will markedly improve. Some managers may feel that keeping their subordinates striving for their approval is a good motivator, but we've found that encouragement and subtle coaching are much more effective.

Accepting people's best efforts is a big part of that. Sometimes the job doesn't get done the way you would have done it. It may not even be up to your standards, but you aren't going to get a better effort the next time around by berating them. Instead, try coaching them with little tips as to how you would improve the job then send them on their way. You'll be surprised how far a little positive push can go.

> "I can live two months on one good compliment."
>
> —*Mark Twain*

If you don't help your people along, they'll never get to that next level. They'll never become the quality leaders tomorrow's fire service is going to need. If nothing is ever good enough for you, then eventually they'll just throw their hands in the air and give up. Instead, try to search for some insight into why you love the job. Instill that love of the job in your young firefighters. Help them to become better firefighters and better people. You'll find that you're not only improving your subordinates, but you're becoming a better leader in the process.

11
INTEREST

Interest is closely tied to insight. A leader must be genuinely interested in what's going on. We love to see officers at our presentations. We present at lots of conferences and we can tell you from personal experience, it helps you stay on the cutting edge of the fire service. Instead of being hung up on a golf course somewhere trying to improve their handicaps, these chiefs and company officers are out there among the troops, trying to learn the best new techniques and tactics. Those officers will make everybody around them better because they'll take that cutting edge information home and teach it to the rest of their people.

We find that those same types of officers are the ones who really know what's going on in their departments. They take a sincere interest in the lives of their firefighters. You can always tell when officers are just going through the motions. They ask a question like, "How are the kids doing?" But they have no idea whether you even have kids, much less how many or how old. We've all dealt with that type of officer. As a leader, you have to be genuinely interested in what's going on in your city and your company, and with your people.

They take a sincere interest
in the lives of their firefighters.

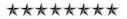

When there's an incident within your department, go talk to the people who know best about it. If you are genuinely interested in the lives of your subordinates, then you can go to them and ask, "What's going on? I heard the last time you worked that you said the saw blades were no good, that they were kicking back? Tell me what happened."

When things happen, follow up. Not only are these issues important to your firefighters, but something that happens in one firehouse in your battalion could just as easily happen at another. It might even happen at the firehouse where you work. Some firefighters just leave the firehouse at the end of the shift and that's that. They don't want any involvement outside of showing up for their work. We're not saying that leaving the firehouse and going home to a life that is separate from your fire department life is a bad thing, but you have to maintain some connection beyond just working your shift. You run that firehouse, so you've got to give it 100%, right?

Everyone has different issues going on in their lives. You have your private life, your fire department life, and maybe even another business or career apart from firefighting. It can be hard to juggle all of them, so you have to compartmentalize.

When I go to work, I walk straight in to the firehouse and right up to my office. If the battalion is out, I take a shower and change into my uniform. If the battalion is in, I quickly locate the chief that I'm relieving and we talk. We'll usually exchange some information; maybe talk about what has happened during the tour. That conversation will usually last anywhere from ten to forty minutes, depending on what's going on.

When I walk to my locker, I take John Salka off and hang him up in the locker. Then I take my uniform and I put on Chief Salka. That's who I become for that shift. As long as I'm wearing that uniform, I'm not John Salka and none of John Salka's problems are in my head.

I don't think about the chlorine in my backyard pool. I don't think about the broken tree branch hanging over my house. I don't worry about my gutters being full of leaves or my front lawn not growing in—I don't worry about any of that.

When I'm at work, I spend twenty-four hours thinking about that firehouse. I'm not thinking about anything but the work and the people in the firehouse. I'm not thinking about anything but work and going out on jobs. I'm thinking about training, safety, and whatever else that firehouse needs to work on. That's how I work. I pay strict attention to my job.

There are some people who can take that too far. When they go home, all they can think about is their jobs. They can't focus on their family, and that can be very destructive. I've found that the key to avoiding that pitfall is to compartmentalize.

When I go home, I take off the uniform and leave Chief Salka in the locker. I put back on my regular clothes and John Salka heads home. I climb into my pickup, and I don't think too much about how many crewmembers are on the engine or what jobs are going on in the Bronx.

While I'm at home, I concentrate on the things I need to do there. I compartmentalize my life very well so that wherever I am at the time, I'm 100% there. Now of course there are emergencies. I don't mean that I'll ignore a call from the firehouse if I'm at home. If something goes on there that I need to know about, they'll call me at home and ask, "Is the Chief there?" Then I have to deal with it; however, I've made it clear to my officers that it should be a serious situation if they call me at home. It has to be something very serious for them to cross that line.

When things are done that way, it allows you to pour yourself into whatever you want. If you chase two rabbits, both will escape. What that really means is don't try to do two things at once because you won't do either one very well. I try to limit myself to one activity. When I'm at work, that's where my focus is: 100%. When I'm at home, that gets 100% of my attention and interest. That way I'm a better leader in the firehouse as well as a better husband and father at home.

"Find a purpose and your passion
will follow."

—*Mac Anderson*

FOCUS!

Have you ever worked with someone who reminded you of Tigger from *Winnie the Pooh*, someone who just seems to bounce off the walls, who can never focus on a single task for very long? We've all seen firefighter like that. They walk into the firehouse with golf clubs over one shoulder, a yachting magazine under one arm, and the previous day's stock market numbers under the other. They're working toward getting a boat; they're polishing their golf clubs; they're talking about the stocks they're invested in; they're doing anything and everything, *except* thinking about the job.

They're not thinking about going to a fire that night; they're not playing through scenarios in their heads, trying to figure out the best methods for their current team; they're definitely not thinking about any of the other multiple issues that go on at any given fire department at any time. Those firefighters are overlapping the different parts of their lives. They're not compartmentalizing, and everything is getting confused with everything else. They're not just chasing one rabbit; they're going after three or four. Those people will never have real success at anything they're doing because they're trying to do everything at once. They're not giving their interest over completely to any one thing, so instead they're getting partial results for a partial effort.

Another good reason to separate the various areas of your life from one another is so that you can have an oasis: a safe zone where you can get away from all your other problems (fig. 11–1).

The firehouse can be your oasis. A lot of times it's hard to separate yourself from what's going on in your outside life. Being a young, single firefighter has its own set of issues; a young married firefighter has others. Being a young father or mother *definitely* carries problems with it. The point is, you're always going to have issues in your personal life. If you are able to keep your private and professional lives separate, then you can use the firehouse as an escape to get away from all those problems. It can be a place where you go to relax and get away from the crying baby or the home improvement list. It can almost feel like you're on another planet, which is a very nice thought for some fire-fighters with hectic home lives.

Fig. 11–1. The firehouse can be a place where you go to escape the rest of your problems. Pictured is Charlotte (NC) Firehouse #39.

Many, many years ago, when I was leaving to serve as the fire chief of Coeur d'Alene, I turned to my old friend Chief Tom Freeman for advice (fig. 11–2).

I said, "Tom, I've done everything. I've worked very hard and now I'm about to 'hang a five' on my collar. What advice can you give me? I need a gold leadership nugget that I can use as I become a chief. I'm moving to Idaho, clear across the country. I won't be right next to you anymore, able to run over and ask for advice whenever I need it."

Fig. 11–2. Chief Tom Freeman, Lisle-Woodridge (IL) Fire Protection District

At the time, my chief was a mutt, big time. The kind of chief who doesn't trust anybody; the kind who hates his guys, and uses his position of power to harass and demean his people. Simply put: he just didn't get it. Tom pointed right across the room at him and said, "Do everything the opposite of that guy and you should do well." I laughed, and he said, "No, I'm serious. Do everything the opposite of (him). You just went through boot camp for fire chiefs. No classroom will ever teach you what you learned working for that guy!"

I hate to be negative, but sometimes you can learn just as much from a cautionary tale as you can from a positive experience. Since I became chief, I've done everything the opposite of that guy and so far it's worked! And worked well! One of the main things that Tom taught me was to treat people like family, like you'd want to be treated. The other guy thought he was God's gift to the fire service and never lowered himself to talk to the little guys. He got promoted and forgot where he came from.

TAKE THE GOOD WITH THE BAD

That's a really good lesson that sometimes is tough to learn. While you can learn a lot from the great leaders you work under, you can also learn a lot from the mutts. It's easy to learn from the good examples. When you agree with someone and consider that person a mentor, it's not very difficult to take their lessons as insightful and instructive.

It's a lot harder to learn from the leaders who don't really care. There are some people who lost the fire a long time ago and are just in it for the paycheck. They spend their free time counting down the months and days until they can retire. Not only should you emulate the actions of the successful folks, you also need to look at the people who aren't doing a good job and say to yourself, "There are some things I want to be sure to avoid."

We've both done that several times. There was a lieutenant I worked under a long time ago. He was a lieutenant when I was a young firefighter working on a truck. He was a great guy and a great tactical officer. This guy was in the FDNY during the busy years. He's retired now, but he was a senior lieutenant when I was just a young firefighter.

This officer could do anything he wanted to. He was very successful and talented, but he was a moody guy. When you came in to work for this officer, everybody asked the same question. As soon as you walked in the firehouse door, you'd look around to see if he was there. If he wasn't, you asked the first person you could find, "Who's the boss today? Is he in yet? How does he look today?"

If the guy answered, "He's great," then phew! No problem.

Other days you'd walk in and the guy would say, "He's having a bad day today." On those days, if I heard him walking down the stairs I'd go into the phone booth and close the door until he passed by. Then I would head upstairs.

I'm not sure if this officer was bipolar or what, but if he wasn't in a good mood it was bad news for the entire firehouse. Now I loved working with him, but you can see how that type of leadership in the firehouse can negatively affect the whole environment.

Here's the boss man. He's setting the tone for the entire firehouse that day. If he was in a good mood, he was one of the best officers to work under; however, if he was in a bad mood, it could damage the morale of everyone there.

One of the good ways to avoid being "that guy" is to talk things through. Every time you're faced with a problem or difficulty, every time you're challenged, don't just let it gnaw away at you. Try to look at the big picture. Even if it's something negative, you can find lessons in the experience. It's not a setback, it's a test.

Try to tell yourself, "This is happening for a reason. There is a lesson here that I'm going to use somewhere down the road. It may happen three hours or three years from now, but I'm going to be ready when it comes."

You may have been sitting in the big chair for twenty years, and you'll still be able to think back to how one captain or another lieutenant used to do things when you were a rookie. Sometime later on in life, those negative experiences will turn into positives, but only if you're willing to learn from them. That's where interest comes back into play. If you take an interest in every aspect of the fire service, not just the fun parts, then you'll end up a much better officer for it.

"Enthusiasm finds the opportunities, and energy makes the most of them."

—*Henry Hoskins*

12
INSPIRATION

I lost a lot of good friends on 9/11. There isn't a firefighter I know who wouldn't turn back the hands of time and stop that terrible event if that were possible; however, I made a conscious decision that I wasn't just going to let my friends end up on a plaque somewhere. When everyone else talks about 9/11, they list all the horrible things that happened. I like to try to take something positive out of it that we can use. I owe that to my friends who sacrificed so much.

Whether we like to admit it or not, 9/11 did a lot for us. Hopefully out of every tragedy something positive comes out. We never used to get funding for anything. I've been to meetings where chiefs are complaining about how it takes six months to clear a Homeland Security grant for new equipment. I always like to ask them how long it took before September 11. The answer is, "A lot longer, if at all."

Some other things changed that day: We started calling each other "brother" and "sister" a lot more often. We hugged each other more than we used to. People got along better in general after the tragedy. That goodwill still carries over to this day. We may have slacked off a little bit, but it's still there and because of the sacrifices that were made, we're better off (fig. 12–1).

I saw sixteen-year-old boys hugging their dads, which is *not* a cool thing to do, you know, if you're a sixteen-year-old boy. People were just much more open after that day.

Fig. 12–1. What did 9/11 do for the fire service?

Ninety-two percent of the departments in this country had no emergency management plan before 9/11; New Orleans was a huge mess during Katrina. They lacked planning and without a plan, well, we all remember.

After 9/11, we've improved in a lot of areas. We have some better equipment. We have more personnel due to some grants. We have been able to give the troops more training because of funding from the state and federal levels. We've also picked up some things that have made the job safer for all of us because of the sacrifices made that day.

Just look at how we respond to large-scale incidents and disasters now. We've gotten better at mutual and automatic aid. We're helping each other a lot more and sharing resources (fig. 12–2).

Fig. 12–2. Nursing home patients are evacuated during a hurricane in Texas. The task took the help of multiple agencies working together, side by side.

That was a horrible, horrible event. No matter who we talk to, they all refer to 9/11 as the worst day in our history. Hopefully, that will remain the worst day, and we don't see more deadly terrorist attacks in the future.

We just all seemed to appreciate each other a little more after that. We all had to face the realization that we might not be around tomorrow. In our job, you have no idea what the next shift holds for you. After 9/11, firefighters all over the country seemed to take that to heart just a little bit more.

Not only did we take care of each other a little more, we also seemed to take a little more pride in the job. None of us knows what comes after death, but we may get to see those people we lost again someday. We aren't saying that there was reasoning behind 9/11, but everything happens for a reason. If we do get to see those firefighters again someday, we don't want to have to tell them that they died in vain. If we don't learn from that day, then they will have died in vain.

There was a general who—following a war—was asked, "Do you think things will ever get back to normal?" He responded, "We'll get back to normal, but normal will have changed." One thing that hasn't changed, however, is our attitude about what we do as public servants.

ONCE A FIREFIGHTER, ALWAYS A FIREFIGHTER

We did this program down in Annapolis for one of the graduating classes. For that particular program, we added a slide to the presentation showing a fire truck and an aircraft carrier to draw a connection between the military and the fire service. There are a lot of parallels between the two. There is the similarity in rank structures. We both follow a hierarchical structure. Both services wear uniforms so that they can be easily identified. They even share the trait of various battalions, engines, or platoons having unit numbers.

We both go to battle every day, facing unexpected situations. The work that both services do is highly dangerous. Both spend a lot of time training and preparing for what is usually a short, high-impact event. Training in the military and fire service share a lot of techniques; the parallels worked great with the young graduating class.

When we talk about the Marine Corps, it hits pretty close to home. Two of my sons are U.S. Marines, and one is an Iraq veteran. When I talk about Marines in my leadership programs, my personal connection helps me understand even more the relationship between the Marines and the fire service. I remember driving down the road one day. In front of me was an old, beat up car that had a bumper sticker on it that read, "Once a Marine, Always a Marine!" (fig. 12–3).

Fig. 12–3. The emblem of the United States Marine Corps

The guy was driving really slowly, doing something like twenty-five in a fifty mile-per-hour zone. I wasn't thrilled with him at the time because I was stuck behind him. Eventually, once I was able to pass him, I saw he was a very old guy, probably eighty-five years old. He had silver hair and a red Marine Corps baseball cap on, and he was just chugging down the road in his old car.

This guy had bought in to the Marine Corps ideology, completely. He had a Marine Corps emblem on his bumper, and a Marine Corps emblem on his hat. He was a Marine for life, until they buried him in the ground. We should feel the exact same way! We should feel the passion for the fire service the way Marines feel a passion for the military service. As a matter of fact, I often wonder why we don't feel even stronger about it than the Marines do.

They build up the lifelong connection after a short period of time. Many of them do a couple of tours and then go on to do other things with their lives, but they never lose that connection to the brotherhood. We spend twenty, twenty-five, even thirty years in the service during our careers. Why wouldn't our connection to the fire service be ten times stronger? I believe it should.

Once a firefighter, always a firefighter!

The FDNY has lost firefighters since 9/11. When I've gone to some of those line-of-duty funerals, I always see retired FDNY members in uniform. They may not have a badge any more, but they're at the funeral wearing their full dress uniforms. We have a retired firefighter organization that issues patches for the uniforms, so those firefighters can be seen wearing the FDNY patch with the "retired" panel, or rocker, on it.

The point is, they may be retired five, even ten years, but they still feel that connection. They still feel like they're a part of the fire department. They show up at line-of-duty funerals and other events wearing their full dress uniforms because they still take pride in their department. If you've read *Pride and Ownership*, then you know a lot of what I'm talking about here. That's a great example of the older generation taking ownership of their department (fig. 12-4). Those retired firefighters don't have to come around anymore. They could just cash that check and sit on a lake somewhere fishing, but they don't. They've taken ownership in their department. They take pride in the way it is represented.

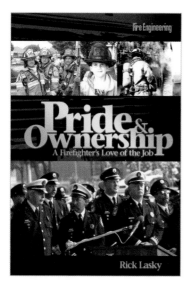

Fig. 12-4. *Pride and Ownership: A Firefighter's Love of the Job* by Rick Lasky

IT'S A CLOSE-KNIT GROUP

No matter where you are, if you're wearing a fire department shirt, you will find other firefighters. It's a law of nature. Some guy will come over and say, "You're a firefighter? I was a firefighter for twenty-two years in East Mudflap, Illinois!"

It doesn't matter where you both worked, you've got something special that you share. Once a firefighter, always a firefighter: Honestly, the only way to get out of the fire service is if we kick your butt out. Whether you were volunteer or paid, you're never done with the fire service. When you retire, whether it was after five years or twenty-five years, you'll always be a firefighter.

Whether you were volunteer or paid,
you're never done with the fire service.

It's always fun to be a part of that group. No matter where you go, you've always got something to talk about. You might be dreading going to that wedding of your spouse's friends because you don't know a single one of them, but as soon as you show up you find out there are two volunteer firefighters there who want to talk shop. Since you share a lot of the same experiences, it feels like you've known each other forever.

Our wives both hate it when we go to weddings or banquets, even if it's not really a fire department function. Inevitably, there will be another firefighter there and our wives won't get a single minute of attention. Even though it may upset your significant other from time to time, you can take inspiration from your membership in the fire service. It's a club with a demanding acceptance policy. It takes a special kind of person to do what we do. Because of that, we should all feel special about the job we get to do every day.

YOUR ATTITUDE IS YOUR CHOICE

It doesn't matter what happened to you yesterday. Leave your bad news at home or hang it up in your locker. If something is bothering you, imagine that you're leaving it with your street clothes in your locker. Leave all that stuff behind and go downstairs and be a part of your group for the duration of the shift.

You may not control anything else, but your attitude is your choice today. As a matter of fact, it's probably one of the few things you can control. You can decide whether you want to have a good attitude or a bad attitude every day of your life. If you let the bad attitude win, if you let those other negative things in your life pull you down, it can then affect your work. That's not fair to the other firefighters on your rig. Everybody has some negative stuff going on in their lives. Nobody goes through life without some struggles. It's the people who let those struggles define them that are eventually going to fail.

> "No matter what happened to you yesterday, your attitude today is your choice."
>
> *—Kent Lenard*

We all have some areas of our lives we wish were going better. It may be a long-term goal or a short-term problem, but everyone has areas they want to improve. The hard part is leaving those issues in the locker. Just put those worries in the closet for a while and have a positive attitude while you're working. If you're a lieutenant, a captain, or a leader of any kind, how you act will trickle down. It will affect everyone you work with. If you have a negative attitude, you will then end up instilling it in your troops.

That's why you need to have a positive attitude all the time. Positive attitudes will make your life better. You'll find that firefighters with positive attitudes enjoy being around the firehouse more. They won't drag around at lunch, trying to stay out longer. They take pride in keeping the firehouse clean in case there's a surprise inspection or a visit from the public. Whatever the areas may be, we believe you'll find a positive attitude at the top will make for a better working environment all around. Eventually, you'll start to influence everyone around and the whole place will start to liven up.

We've all worked with Eeyore, the donkey from *Winnie the Pooh* before, right? We call him Eeyore because the minute you see him you wish he would just go away. You're just sitting there in the kitchen, minding your own business and trying to wake up and start the day when he walks in. Immediately he starts complaining, "This place sucks. I hate this. Mornings are awful. I just wish I wasn't here." You know the type. When that same negative person gets promoted, he can't understand why nobody wants to follow him.

> "A leader's job is to look into the future and see the organization, not as it is, but as it should be."
>
> —*Jack Welch*

John McCain was a prisoner of war for several years in Vietnam. In a P.O.W. camp, all you've got is your attitude. They've taken everything else away from you. You have no freedom, you're lucky if you get edible food, and you're regularly tortured. Your attitude is all you've got left.

John McCain refused to let the Viet Cong destroy his attitude. While he was in that hellhole, he tells the story of another prisoner who managed to find little scraps of fabric. Over time, he got enough fabric for a makeshift American flag. Every day he and the rest of the prisoners said the Pledge of Allegiance to that flag. Of course the Viet Cong would toss the cells and find the flag. Then they would beat the flag maker unmercifully and leave him badly injured. All the other prisoners would do what they could to patch this guy up and get him going again.

This prisoner had been beaten almost to death, but do you know what he was doing before sunset that very night? Making another flag. All they had was their attitude. He could easily have given up right then and there. They had destroyed the symbol of hope he had labored over. They had beaten him within an inch of his life. They had taken everything they could from those people, but they couldn't destroy their attitudes. Think how lucky we are that we don't have to suffer under conditions like that. The little, everyday problems like paying the bills don't seem quite so big and awful when you compare them to John McCain's experiences in Vietnam.

> "Your attitude toward others often determines their attitude toward you."
>
> —*John Maxwell*

WHAT LITTLE BITS WILL YOU LEAVE BEHIND?

Have you ever walked into a firehouse and said, "Oh my God! How did that lieutenant get to be so negative?" Have you ever worked with someone who had an extremely negative attitude? It just never goes away, does it? Some people are just miserable. You feel bad for the person, but you also have to worry about it spreading to the rest of the company.

Why does one negative attitude spread so efficiently to everyone else around, but ten positive people can't cheer up one grumpy one? It really gets scary when you see it passed on from generation to generation. Let's say you work for one of those people with a chronically negative attitude. One day, after you've been working under such a person for several months, his or her retired captain stops by for coffee. After five minutes you'll see that your negative captain is just a chip off this old block.

What do you want to leave behind for the people who come after you? Someone comes storming in and slams the door, huffs around the firehouse, then sits down and starts to complain. When the other firefighters see that, do you want them to say, "Oh, that's the Salka in him. He trained with John for so long that it rubbed off." Do you want to leave that type of mark on your firehouse, or would you rather be remembered for your good habits. When people see a clean firehouse, respectful firefighters who enjoy their jobs, a spotless rig, and tools so clean you could eat with them, that's when you want them to say, "That was John Salka's doing. He really whipped this place into shape and now they all take pride in the firehouse like he did."

*What do you want to leave behind
for the people who come after you?*

Every one of us takes little bits and pieces of all the people we've worked with throughout our careers. Just take a moment and think of the best officer that you ever worked for. Why was that person the best? And then take another moment and think of the worst officer you ever worked with. Why was that person the worst? What did you take from these officers? When it comes to the good one, hopefully a lot; from the bad one, hopefully only the lessons on what you shouldn't do. Whether you mean to or not, you're constantly leaving behind little cues for the people who will follow you.

A saying we borrowed from one of our friends goes, "If you follow ugly kids home, you're going to find ugly parents." The same thing can be said of firefighters. If you see a crew of firefighters who don't take care of their rig, don't clean their tools, and don't take pride in the uniform, then you can probably find a bad officer leading them.

What does one blue shirt with a positive attitude say to another one with a negative attitude? When I was a firefighter, I felt like I was banging my head against the wall a lot of the time. I didn't know what to do in order to make the other members have a better attitude and start taking care of the firehouse. I had a positive effect on a few of them, but I had to learn that not everyone has the same passion for the job that I do. Not everyone is going to love the job the same. It took a while for me to figure that out. As a regular firefighter, there wasn't much I could do about it because I didn't have a lot of control. All I could do was hope that they transferred out. I did what I could to make positive changes in my circle of influence. I tried to be the go-to guy. Anything I was asked to do, I did without any complaints.

When I got responsibility—I won't say power—but, when I was finally promoted to a place where I could make a difference, I started to use these same skills we've been discussing.

I would call up a mentor and ask, "Why am I having such a problem with this issue? Why doesn't my team get what I'm trying to teach them?" I used my network to make changes I thought would be positive for the company.

I've got a unique way to deal with those negative problems these days. It's another technique I've picked up from somebody else along the way. Chief Curtis Birt is a good friend of mine (fig. 12–5). Whenever he had one of those chronic complainers come through his firehouse, he had a method to deal with the situation.

Fig. 12–5. Lake Cities (TX) Chief Curtis Birt

Curtis would sit the negative member down and say, "Why do you hate working here so much? Do you want to be here? If not, we can fix that!" Curtis would then take a folder out and sit down at the kitchen table with the complaining firefighter. That folder would be full of applications for a bunch of local employers. He would say, "Come on. Let's sit down and fill one of these applications out. Put me down as a reference. I'll even drive you there and tell them what a great employee you are!"

Nobody ever took him up on it, but sometimes you've got to give somebody a little bop-on-the-nose to get their attention. I've used that same method many times. I'll sit down with the guy and say, "Look, I've got nowhere to put you. Because of your attitude, none of the other shifts want you. Even the people around here who have put up with you don't want to work with you anymore."

When you say that to firefighters, it's like ripping their hearts out. It can be tough, but sometimes as a leader you need to be willing to step up and tell people how far out of place they are.

Almost every time I've had to do this, they deny it. They'll swear up and down they don't hate work, it's just that they have an issue. Maybe they were passed over for promotion before I even showed up, but they've been holding on to the anger over it for years.

Sometimes you'll find the root of the problem and work it out. Every once in a while, you'll get someone who just doesn't have a love of the job. They don't have the same passion that most of us share, and you will have to send that person off to the land of the clay people, as I call it.

USE UNITY

Sometimes it can be hard to stay positive. The more responsibility you get, the more problems you will have to deal with. We can guarantee that you are going to have some problems. You will have unmotivated firefighters. You will have distracted firefighters. It's your job to do what you can to fix the situation.

Usually a good talk is all it will take to improve matters. No firefighter, no person, enjoys being the outcast. As soon as you point out how much of a burden the person has become, nearly anyone will go out of their way to remedy the situation—Well almost anyone!

Sometimes you can use the firefighter's sense of unity to your advantage. Occasionally, some members will lose the passion. We've all seen it. They're good firefighters, but they've been on the job so long it's become routine. They don't enjoy training. They usually just want to sit around and watch television.

A good way to get those types of firefighters to wake up is to appeal to their sense of unity. Give them a project. "You're going to help us with the drill today. You know, the new kids, Karen and Tommy? They need a little bit of help with their roof cutting skills. I'm busy, so could you do me a favor and work with them during the next drill? You've got a lot of time on the job and you've done it a million times, could you handle that for me?"

A good way to get those types of firefighters to wake up is to appeal to their sense of unity.

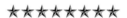

That way you don't make the issue about the firefighters, you make it about the company. You didn't even have to have "the talk" with these firefighters to awaken a sense of inspiration. All you had to do was place them in a situation where they felt like they were a useful part of the team again. You have put them in a position of responsibility where they're able to pass on some of their knowledge.

Sometimes that's all it takes for firefighters who are just feeling a little bit unappreciated. If you drop a little more work on them, they'll respond by working harder. They know you're expecting something more from them and they're happy to rise to the challenge. On top of that, they will usually get a positive feeling out of helping the younger firefighters. At the end of the drill, they'll probably get a "thank you," and a sense of accomplishment from helping improve their company.

13
INTENSITY

What is intensity? It's another very important element of leadership. You have to love the job with intensity and enthusiasm. It will show in your work and spread to your company. When you work with intensity, you get more accomplished. Intensity isn't just about blind energy, going one-hundred miles per hour. It's about getting things done (fig. 13–1). You have to focus your intensity and use it to increase your productivity.

Fig. 13–1. Intensity is about getting things done.

Intensity is that inner attitude you get when you're deeply engaged in the work you do. Your intensity level can greatly affect the intensity level of those around you. Your lack of intensity will also rub off, so always try to be energetic when you're on the job. Even if you're tired, act like you aren't. It will energize your troops which will, in turn, give you more energy.

Pete Lund was one of my officers when I worked in Rescue 3, and over the years we became friends. Pete had tremendous intensity about the FDNY and about working in "the Rescue." Just working with Pete, being on duty when he was riding the front seat, was inspirational. I know I have carried some of that intensity from Pete with me, and I hope I have been able to pass some of it on to the firefighters who have worked with me in my company officer assignments.

IT'S ALL ABOUT HEART

Patton and other great leaders like him spread their intensity to those around them and it helped them achieve positive results. A leader with great passion and few skills always outperforms a leader with great skills but no passion. Passion is everything.

A leader with great passion and few skills always outperforms a leader with great skills but no passion.

If you have a captain assignment open, who do you want to choose to fill it and run that company? Do you want the officer who just does the bare minimum, someone who is never late, but also never early? Someone who doesn't really do much beyond what is required on and off the job? No! You want an officer with a passion for the job in that company. You want the officer whose intensity is displayed every minute of every shift. You want the officer who is always inquisitive, always trying to learn more about the job (fig. 13–2). The spark plug that shows you some passion is the one you want in your house; not the person who got the best exam score and just sits there waiting for someone else to do it all, but the one with the biggest heart.

"When the wind goes out of the sail, the boat drifts with the current."

—*Old sailor's truth*

Fig. 13–2. As a lieutenant, captain, battalion chief, and now as a deputy chief in the FDNY's 7th Division, Jay Jonas has and always will be all about passion, the job, and, most of all, his people.

Passion is also contagious. It brings up your level of efficiency, safety, and professionalism. It can even improve your technical skills. I can teach you how to force a door. I can teach you how to cut a roof. Nobody comes into the department knowing how to cut a roof. Everyone has to be taught. We didn't know how to force a door when we first started and now we're writing books, teaching at conferences, and overseeing promotions. We can teach you how to force a door or cut a roof, but we can't teach passion. Skills are teachable, intensity is not. You can't sit down with someone and explain how to be passionate in a step-by-step process. You can always teach more skills, but somebody has to want to be passionate about the job (fig. 13–3).

You can take someone with tons of passion but few skills and mold that person into a great officer. Try the same thing with a skilled firefighter who lacks passion and you probably won't be so successful.

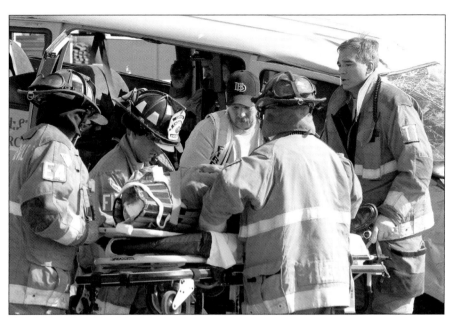

Fig. 13–3. Passion that breeds intensity brings a fire company together, often resulting in the ability to overcome tremendous odds.

"All great achievements have one thing in common—people with a passion to succeed."

—*Pat Cash*

Passion is the only thing that got us through 9/11 (fig. 13–4). There are four or five different operations going on in that picture. Notice how almost everyone in the photo is looking downward. Every operation was very small, no bigger than a throw rug. If you look closely, you can see five different groups working in five distinct areas. Each one was separate from the others.

Fig. 13–4. The tragedy of 9/11 brought out extremely passionate feelings in all of us.

In the first days and weeks, there were literally hundreds of small little areas of operation all over Ground Zero. It had nothing to do with technical expertise at that point. We were digging with garden shovels. We were unable to use big tools because everything was either too heavy, or too wide. They were all interconnected and crushed, so small hand tools were all we could use. Those were some long, tough days. It was all passion that got us through those very difficult times.

14
INFORMATION

Lots of places just give a person a promotion, and that's that. They give you a different colored shirt, a new assignment, and that's the end of the formal training. It's astounding to us that departments take firefighters from their line positions—whether they're riding backwards or a pump operator—and just move them up to lieutenant without any training whatsoever. Our departments put trainees through weeks of training to get them up to snuff before they're actually given a higher level of responsibility, but so many places don't do any officer training at all.

Training for leadership is a huge element of becoming an officer. There are two major parts to being an officer. First there's the tactical area, then there are the less fun administrative duties. As an officer, you will have to deal with performance evaluations, policy reviews, and many other "boring" parts of the job that you don't hear about that much. Just because they aren't glorified doesn't mean they aren't vital to the day-to-day operations of a fire department.

If you look at the amount of time you spend at operations, and compare it to the amount of time you spend doing all the administrative aspects of your job back at the firehouse, the paperwork will outweigh the action ten-to-one. Even in the busiest company in New York City or Los Angeles, the officers only spend a small portion of their time on operations. The rest of the time is spent on evaluations, training, and other administrative duties.

I WISH I'D KNOWN!

Officer training is sorely lacking in many departments around the country. One of the main root causes of that is they have no promotion structure. Lots of volunteer departments just use elections to select officers. While it may sound democratic, that can at times be a weak way to choose your leaders. You may end up with the person who has more in the way of political influence than what is needed to get the job done and lead the department. We've both been volunteer firefighters through the years and have seen how they pick their officers.

Many larger departments will base their promotions on interviews, exams, and demonstrated capabilities. A small committee along with the chief makes decisions on who gets promoted. That's a much more effective way to choose your leaders than just a simple election. That way, you don't end up with the most popular person in charge, you get the most competent.

A lot of people just get promoted or elected to office, but they receive nothing in the way of training and preparation. Not only do they get zero official training, they have no continuing education requirements. The only difference between John Doe the firefighter and John Doe the captain is the color of his shirt. They haven't been taught any other skills that prepare them for this huge new level of responsibility.

We meet people like that all the time. They show up at our lectures and approach us afterward saying, "I wish I'd known that! I've been an officer for three years and they haven't even given me a book or a manual to read. I just went out of the frying pan and into the fire with no guidance whatsoever." A lot of people will say, "That's fine for your big departments like FDNY, but we're a small department, and we can't afford expensive training courses and trips to conventions."

That's not necessarily true. You may not be able to afford a trip to FDIC, but you can afford a book on leadership. You can afford to pick up those one or two books that can get you on the way to doing what you need to do, and that's leading. You don't have to send the entire officer corps to Maui for a two-week, hands-on training course. There are other, less expensive ways to improve your leadership skills. We've seen departments that are 150 years old that don't do any leadership training. They could have three hundred members, but they will still use the small department excuse.

One place that most departments are lacking and that doesn't cost them a dime is mentoring. We just don't see the officers doing what should be their main job: making more officers. They aren't putting in the time with their subordinates in order to grow them into effective officers.

"If everyone below me is successful, then I am!"

It all goes back to the successors. Once you achieve a position of leadership, one of your primary responsibilities is to prepare your successors. If the officers who come after you in the firehouse aren't good leaders, that's your fault. A lot of people just live their lives as officers and do a good job at that aspect, but they never really mentor any of the young future leaders along. Then when they come back to visit and the firehouse is a mess, they wonder where the leadership failed.

If the officers who come after you in the firehouse aren't good leaders, that's your fault.

TAKE A LOOK IN THE MIRROR

If you want to run a successful department in the long term, you have to make a concerted effort to prepare the next generation of leaders. If you know some firefighters scored really high on their exams, and they'll probably be promoted in the next year, then arrange for them to come by your office. Go through some of the paperwork with them. Let them fill out the paperwork and the forms. Get them familiar with the building inspection forms. Start them out on some of the less dangerous aspects of the job so they can get their feet wet. That way, when they get to the office on their first day as lieutenants, they aren't completely overwhelmed by all the little administrative details.

Get them used to the mundane aspects of the job in a familiar environment. It doesn't even have to be an official program. You can institute this type of mentoring in your own office, even if nobody in the rest of the department follows suit. You just have to make a conscious decision to share some of your expertise and time. You'll find that most of the up-and-coming officers are eager to get any information they can about the job. You should be just as eager to share information, and mold them into successful officers.

INFORMATION CAN SAVE LIVES

Information isn't the most exciting topic. Most people hear it and tune out; however, in our line of work, information can be the difference between life and death. Sometimes information is mundane but useful. Passing on information could be as simple as posting a bulletin about the upcoming lieutenant's exam so promotion-minded firefighters can start preparing early. That's information sharing that just takes a second, but can have a major impact on other firefighters' careers. They might not have found out on their own, so by passing along that information, you've been the difference-maker in their success and promotion. Then you've not only helped those young firefighters, but you've improved the entire department by strengthening its leadership structure.

Take a look at figure 14–1. When you start to examine that situation, suddenly you realize how important information can be. Imagine you're that firefighter who's about to enter that window. The next room over is on fire. If information that someone is about to enter the room isn't passed along, then the attack team on the other side of the building won't know to hold back.

"Hold up on the fire attack. I'm going to check the adjacent room real quick. There may be somebody in there. As soon as I jump out you can open the hoseline."

Without that information, the attack team might drive the fire right into the room that this firefighter is searching. That's a little piece of information that would be life saving. Information varies greatly in its importance. Some bits of information, like the example from figure 14–1, are vital to survival. Other information, like what time dinner happens at the firehouse, isn't as important to save lives, but it's still necessary to keep the place running smoothly. So you can see, information affects all levels of the fire service.

Fig. 14–1. Provide your people with the information they need to do their jobs.

Information affects all levels of the fire service.

DON'T SANDBAG!

You have to give your people the information they're going to need to succeed. In our travels around the country, so many times, we'll meet young firefighters and find that we know more about the history of their department than they do. We'll ask, "What happened at that fire in your city a few years ago?" These young firefighters weren't around then, and no one has told them anything about it, so they just say, "I don't know." If we aren't willing to share information, we're going to keep killing firefighters the old fashioned way. We're going to continue to stumble through leadership within the firehouse and it *will* cost lives.

Again, it doesn't have to be operational. We see shortcomings of leadership all the time. How many company officers have been through a good class on performance evaluations? Very few. We can tell you that from experience, but when you turn in an evaluation that's not complete, you can bet you're going to hear about it. How can you get onto someone for not doing the report correctly when you didn't give that person all the information that was needed to do the job? Lots of times, the blame doesn't get placed where it belongs. If your subordinates aren't doing what you want them to, don't blame them. You are responsible for clearly conveying what you want to happen.

Three or four of us used to get together to study for promotion tests. No matter how good of friends we were, there was always a little healthy competition. You have to be careful, though, because competition can turn snippy fast. You start worrying about things like, "What if he passes and I don't? He may be smarter than me, but I don't want the whole world to know. I'm going to sabotage him just a little bit. You know, even out the playing field?"

You can't sandbag like that, especially as a leader. As the leader, you should be giving up literally every tiny piece of information you can pass along. You should hope that the guys you're training get a better score than you. You should do everything in your power to make those younger officers-in-training turn out to be better fire officers than you could ever be.

In Lewisville, we had a program on succession titled, "Line of Sight." Pretty much everyone was trained to the next level. In some cases, whether they wanted to or not. I used to say if I was hit by a bus tomorrow, my two assistant chiefs would be able to step in immediately. They knew how to do my job. They even knew all the little details; nothing was a secret.

But it didn't stop there. Those two assistants had people waiting in the wings who could step in and do their jobs. They'd been training their replacements just like I was training them. They'd been teaching those up-and-comers all the important aspects of the assistant chief's job. Some of it was so subtle they didn't even realize they were being groomed for that next position.

Below that position was division chiefs, and I used to make every one of them give me at least one name of someone they were mentoring to take their jobs from them. Well, you know what I mean, not take their jobs from them, but be ready to step up when that time comes. We took mentoring and made it systemic. Part of being a firefighter in Lewisville is being ready to step up to the next spot if you're needed. It all actually works kind of easy.

FROM FIREFIGHTER TO DRIVER ENGINEER

As a firefighter gets to a point where he or she feels ready to "bump up" or "act up," or when the captain feels the firefighter is ready, the captain submits this request to the battalion chief, who then submits it to the training division. The member is then given study material for the written exam and a time frame for completion. After completing and passing the written exam, a driving and pumping practical follows. Both require a passing grade, and there is plenty of time given to practice for both. The process for a member to be approved as an acting driver engineer also requires a written exam along with a pumping and driving practical. The driving practical is the same one given during the promotional process, and the pumping practicals are similar. When all is completed, the training division submits the member for approval by the chief of operations to serve in the acting driver engineer role.

FROM DRIVER ENGINEER TO CAPTAIN

Just as it works with the firefighter acting as driver engineer, this process starts off the same way with a request or recommendation to act up as captain. The promotional process for captain involves a written exam, a tactical assessment, and an in-basket exercise. The process for a member to be approved for acting capabilities is pretty much the same. The member is given a written exam, a tactical assessment involving a single-family dwelling fire, and several in-basket exercises dealing with the types of scenarios a shift captain would face. After passing all portions of the exam, the results are sent to the chief of operations for approval.

FROM CAPTAIN TO BATTALION CHIEF

This one is similar to the one described above for a driver engineer to act up as captain, except it is tailored more for the multicompany officer. The tactical assessment involves a multifamily dwelling fire with several challenges and in-basket exercises that hit on the types of situations that a battalion chief would handle. In addition to these requirements, the candidate has to "ride out" with the battalion chief for a minimum of three shifts. During this time the battalion chief and the captain can switch roles, allowing for the captain to act up as battalion chief and the battalion chief to serve as the "coach."

Our division and assistant chiefs are often working with each other in an effort to prepare each for that next level. The idea is not to hold anything back. Again, as stated earlier, too many officers are afraid to share what they know with those coming up under them because "they might just end up knowing as much as I do." I thought that was what we wanted to do in the first place. It's the only way to make it all better. We're giving them the information early. We don't just wait until a month before the promotion exam and start cramming. Members of my fire department were being prepared for the next level of succession from the time they start the last one. If it works, then I should be the last outside fire chief they should have to hire (fig. 14–2).

Fig. 14–2. Lewisville Assistant Chiefs Darrell Brown and Tim Tittle define the word loyalty and could step in and take my job as chief at any moment and not miss a beat. Darrell is now with the Grapevine (TX) FD and Tim is now the fire chief in Lewisville.

THE NEXT GENERATION GETS THE SHADE

The mentoring process is a long, tedious process. You'll probably see some immediate results, but the big changes you're working towards may not come during your career. We're used to our wireless networks, our smart phones, all the immediately available information of today. We get frustrated with the fire service nowadays because things don't happen at the rapid pace we want. Sometimes good stuff can take a while.

When you ask people what the biggest problem is in the fire service, many will answer, "resistance to change." That's true across the board, and it comes from our heritage. The fire service, as an institution, is extremely proud of its heritage. That's a great thing. We're both big proponents of history, as you've seen in this book. Still, a reverence for history doesn't preclude a willingness to change for the better. You also have to learn to be patient. Change won't happen overnight. In many cases, you won't be instituting change for your own benefit, but for future generations of firefighters. There's an old saying that goes, "one generation plants the trees while the other gets the shade."

How many older people do you know have a deviated septum because, when they were infants, we didn't enforce child car seat laws? You just sat on mom or dad's lap when you rode around in the car. When they slammed on the breaks, guess what happened? You hit your nose on the dashboard, and now you've got a little piece of your nose that's still crooked to this day. Today, they won't even let you leave the hospital with a newborn unless you've got a child seat. It seems like a commonsense thing, but how long did it take to get those laws enacted?

THE LEADER WHO WAS THERE BEFORE YOU

The best place to find information about the next job in your line is to talk to the person who's already doing that job. There is no better place to get information about a job you're going to do than from an experienced leader who has already done it. Talk to that person and learn as much as you can before promoting.

It's a good idea to practice what we refer to as "the battalion chief bubble." That's where a captain who is getting ready to promote to chief rides around with several different chiefs to get an idea of what the job is like. The trainee enters "the battalion chief bubble" and gets hands-on experience as well as different perspectives on the job.

Those candidates for promotion always get excited, and it's fun to watch. They aren't junior members of the department. They are captains or lieutenants, experienced officers, but they're getting ready to jump into the whole new realm of the battalion chief. Whether it's a firefighter getting ready to go to company officer, or a company officer getting ready to proceed to chief officer, they all enjoy learning from more experienced, senior officers. It can also encourage and excite you as a senior officer to pass on what you've learned.

The fire service, as an institution, is extremely proud of its heritage.

In the FDNY, we have something called the New York State First Line Supervisor Training Program. Every professional fire officer in the state of New York who gets promoted has to spend several weeks going through the statewide program. Volunteers don't take part, but every last career officer from every department goes there to get information about leadership. It's a tremendous program.

Most places don't have anything similar. They just give you your next assignment and tell you to show up on Monday.

Obviously, there's a lot you can learn from courses like that, but you can learn even more of the on-the-job, unofficial requirements by riding around with the person who is currently doing the job you hope to start.

One of my good friends, Tom Kennedy, was a battalion chief with the 16th Battalion in Harlem. He ended up making deputy chief and retired a few years ago, but when he worked in the 16th battalion he was a very senior battalion chief. When the FDNY sent a captain to ride with Tom for training, he'd sit in the back, and have the captain ride the front seat and really experience the chief's role. He wasn't trying to act fancy, like he had a chauffeur. He was training. Tom would let the captain get on the radio, talk to the dispatcher, take telephone messages, request updates on assignments, give signals on the radio, talk to company officers and firefighters at incidents over walkie-talkies. He would let them do the whole thing—the whole battalion chief experience.

Tom was always there and ready to step in if something happened that the captain couldn't handle, but he tried to let the trainee handle most situations on his or her own. When those captains finally got promoted to battalion chief, it was no big deal. They'd handled the job of a battalion chief several times with the expert guidance of a senior "mentor." The promotion was just a formality.

THE PAYOFF

If you have a good mentoring program set up, it can ease the transition during promotion. If you've already seen all the little things, such as building inspections, taking over the new position can be a lot less stressful. You start to get a handle on all the job requirements before you even start. Lots of recently promoted officers spend the first weeks and months after a promotion fretting about what's coming next. They worry that they're not doing the job right and some officer is going to call them out on it. They worry that they won't be ready for the next big fire.

If you've taken part in a good mentoring program, most of those worries are washed away. You've spent the last few weeks or months learning exactly what the job entails; there aren't any big surprises. You've already seen all the positive and negative aspects of the job and you're mentally prepared to handle them adequately.

Another benefit of a mentoring program is that it can help you build up your professional network. We talked earlier about the importance of having a healthy professional network you can turn to for advice. If you're being mentored, either by someone in your company or an outside officer, be sure to make a connection there so you can contact that person later if you need to.

Sometimes you just need confirmation that your thinking is on the right path. You need someone you can call and say, "Hey, Tom. I just wanted to run something by you. I'm not crazy here, am I?" Tom will usually say, "No, you're right on." Other times, your network might stop you from making a mistake by telling you you're heading down the wrong path. That brings up another important point: people in your network have to be honest with you. If you call someone and ask what he or she thinks, you want to hear honest beliefs so you can avoid stepping on any land mines. Yes-people won't teach you anything.

When there is good information sharing, it improves the overall quality of the department's organizational culture. When you start mentoring tomorrow's successors, you improve the whole department for the long haul. You're also helping people. Mentoring brings up promotion rates, which raises salaries, which improves the lives of firefighters, so there are several different places you can improve the department through mentoring.

When you start mentoring tomorrow's successors,
you improve the whole department for the long haul.

WHAT DO YOU WANT TO BE WHEN YOU GROW UP?

It's not just officers who can be mentors, either. There are coaches in all different areas of the fire department. The Lewisville Fire Department has a dive-rescue program that includes 56 divers. That program needs mentors. Most departments have an arson investigation unit. That's another program that will need good mentors. Those aren't the type of jobs you can just figure out on your own. It takes specialized training and a large skill set to perform them at a high level. Without a good mentor, you probably won't ever become a good arson investigator. The point is, you may not know what specialization you want to take in your career. A good mentor can not only make that decision easier, but also help turn an average firefighter into an elite member of a special operations team.

TRUST

The mentor position is one of trust, and that goes both ways. You can't go down to the kitchen and say, "This captain that's mentoring me really doesn't know what he's talking about." That's a breach of trust. By the same token, the captain can't walk into the firehouse and call his replacement an idiot for not filling out a building inspection form correctly.

Both people in that relationship are probably going to learn some things about the other that they would rather not have broadcast on the evening news. Besides, if the people around you see you breaking the trust of another firefighter, then they're going to learn that you aren't a trustworthy person.

You want to be an active mentor. If there are young firefighters coming up and they're looking for someone to guide them, who are they going to choose? Will they pick the battalion chief who doesn't write any articles, isn't involved in training, and doesn't teach at any academies? Or will they choose the chief who takes part in all those activities and more?

Of course they're going to choose the second chief. When we are looking for someone to emulate, we look to the person who is successful, who has good communication skills, and who is good at dealing with people. Nobody wants to spend time with the wallflower who sits at a desk all day and never really talks to anyone.

You have to pick the right person to be your mentor. Someone who has a passion for teaching and helping others. Someone who lives for the job. Someone who has integrity and intensity and all the other "I" words we've discussed. The mentor doesn't have to be a genius or be able to speak five languages, as long as he or she can speak firefighter. You have to find someone who is a good communicator and a good motivator, which is usually pretty easy if you're highly motivated yourself. A mentor needs to show a willingness to help. Anyone who has done some mentoring like we both have will know it's not a one-way street. The mentor gets a lot out of that relationship, too. Just because you've promoted to chief doesn't mean you know everything there is to know about being a captain, lieutenant, or firefighter. There is always more to learn. Being a mentor is a good way to stay connected to the younger generation.

If you want to stay on top of the latest trends, then become a mentor. Where is the best place to have a surgical procedure? It's usually a teaching hospital because they will use the most cutting edge medical techniques. The same thing goes for the fire service. Where is the best place to learn the newest techniques in firefighting? At a fire academy. There you have not only the old guard, but fresh, inquisitive minds coming in that challenge the way we normally approach problems. When those two powerful forces meet, the entire learning process is enhanced and everybody benefits.

CHALLENGES

Mentoring presents its own set of challenges, but they all share the same root causes: attitude, beliefs, and values. If you're dealing with someone who has a bad attitude, you're going to have a challenge. Remember when we talked about Eeyore? He's the one nobody wants to see coming because he has nothing but negative things to say. Trying to mentor someone like that can be very difficult.

That doesn't mean you shouldn't try, though. Just because some people aren't pleasant doesn't mean they can't make positive contributions. Lots of firefighters have poor people skills. I'm sure we all know an officer who was more knowledgeable in an area of expertise than anyone else on the planet, but was as abrasive as sandpaper. You have to be willing to get through that rough exterior to find the person's usefulness, but it's worth it. Underneath are some of the most dedicated, intelligent fire officers in the country.

That being said, people skills are vitally important for those of us in leadership roles. You could have the smartest officer in the world, but if that intelligence is paired with terrible people skills, no one will listen to the officer's brilliant ideas. You don't want to chase anyone off because they're a poor communicator, but you should definitely take it into account when you're considering who to promote.

You have to be willing to get through that rough exterior to find the person's usefulness, but it's worth it.

★★★★★★★★

When you're looking at your department and trying to decide who to promote, don't feel obliged to automatically take the most senior firefighters or the most intelligent ones. If they have poor people skills, you might want to move on to other candidates. People who have great people skills and a genuine passion for the job will make better leaders than those who have all the smarts in the world but can't communicate.

If you are mentoring someone, and that person comes to you and identifies a personal problem or weakness, that information has to remain confidential. A good mentor needs to be trustworthy. If you undermine that trust, you can sabotage the entire relationship. For the most part, confidentiality is a given. Neither one of us has to tell our staff, "keep this between us." When personal information is discussed, it's understood that we all will keep it private.

A good mentor needs to be trustworthy.

A mentor is like a tutor. If you sent your kid to a math tutor after school, you'd be upset if you saw that same tutor at the coffee shop saying, "Man, that kid I just got through with was an idiot!" There may not be any legal confidentiality with a tutor, but you would expect that sort of information to be kept private. If not, you would probably find another tutor.

> "What you see here, what you say here, what you hear here, when you leave here, let it stay here!"

While you're mentoring, you're going to see and hear a lot of stuff about your students. You will see some abilities and skills that may not be up to snuff, but that's why you're there. You're there to help solve the problems, not to gossip about them to everybody else.

Other times the challenges might be internal. We've seen some great people get to positions where their egos got out of control. There are chiefs who could have the cure for cancer, but city hall wouldn't listen to them because of the size of their egos. You can't take yourself too seriously. As soon as you start to hold yourself above other people, you're going to have problems.

We're the two least perfect people we know. All we want to do with this book is offer something that you can take with you. Some of you might read this and say, "Well, that was a waste of time." Others may have already known most of what they've read, but they can use this book as a confirmation that they were doing the right thing already. Even if you're already doing the right thing, it's always nice to hear it from somebody else. We just hope that we've passed along at least a few things that you will find useful in your career.

STRIKE A BALANCE

Sharing information through a mentoring process does a lot of good. Anyone who has done any mentoring in their fire department knows that there is great value to it. What we don't talk about as much is the cost involved. When your captains are riding around with the chief, they aren't on the line leading their companies. Others to fill in for them, which often costs overtime and creates extra budgetary concerns. If your department is going to take up a mentoring program, you have to learn to strike a balance between the needs of the department as a whole and the needs of the mentoring program.

Smaller departments probably aren't going to be able to start a full-fledged program like the FDNY has in operation. It's just not financially feasible. But you don't have to do it that way; there are a lot of ways to practice mentoring (fig. 14–3).

Fig. 14–3. Mentoring can take place anytime, in the firehouse and on the fireground.

If a firefighter were about to get promoted, sometimes the officers would let the person get a taste of the new role ahead of time. Let's say that everybody knew this guy Joe is getting promoted. It's already gone through, it's just a matter of time for it to become official. About a week before he actually gets promoted, the officer will let him ride up in the front seat.

We've seen lieutenants sitting in the back on the irons. It's confused us when the truck pulls up to a fire and I see a captain with a set of irons and the firefighter with a flashlight.

That's a situation where it's okay to stretch the rules a little bit. Both of the roles are staffed, so no one is going out on runs shorthanded. They're getting this young officer some real-time experience in the new position. You don't have to have a huge, department-wide mentoring program. It certainly doesn't hurt, and I'd recommend it wholeheartedly, but you don't need it to be an effective mentor.

Mentoring can be done right in the firehouse where a chief and a company officer, captain, and lieutenant work together. A lot of unofficial mentoring can go on every day if you just pull some young firefighters aside and talk to them a little bit. Your senior officers can do the same thing with captains and lieutenants. Just pull them aside every once in a while and impart a little bit of knowledge. It doesn't have to be anything big. Just say, "When you get promoted to lieutenant, you're going to have to do this. When I had to do it, it worked well this way." Little nuggets of valuable information can go a long way.

HOW TO GAUGE SUCCESS

If you are able to start mentoring, either in a large-scale program or on a one-to-one basis, it will make your fire department more efficient and save you money. Again, you don't have to have some massive program in order to make a difference. It definitely makes it easier, but it's not a requirement for success. It doesn't have to be a big deal where firefighters are required to leave their firehouse or work extra shifts. A mentoring program can be something you implement in between runs, just a little bit of time dedicated to pass on some information to the people coming after you. Your success isn't gauged by your accomplishments, but by the success of the firefighters that come after you. If they fail, then you have failed. If they succeed, then you were also a success.

You don't have to have some massive program
in order to make a difference.

Now we don't mean to say that just because you sit around the table and shoot the breeze with the firefighters, it makes you a good mentor as an officer. It's important to stay connected to your team, but just because you know all their kids' names doesn't make you an effective mentor.

I've already talked about the successful mentoring program we have in Lewisville. I wrote an article in *Fire Engineering* (July 2002) that really outlines the whole program and explains the guts of what we've done there. You don't necessarily have to go that far, but you do have to be willing to really put some effort into it.

Just to say you have a mentoring program, because your firefighters like to sit around and chat on Sundays, may be stretching the truth a bit.

I recently taught a class for a friend of mine. At his department, they have a six-month long mentoring program. When a new firefighter comes on the job, the or she is assigned to a senior firefighter. From the time the two walk in the door, they do everything together. They work the same stations and shifts. Their third night on the job, both firefighters' families are invited for a dinner with the chiefs to talk about the job. It's a very extensive program.

You walk into one of his firehouses, and there will be one of the senior officers saying, "Come with me, Probie. Stick with me and I'll tell you how things work around here." It's just automatic. As soon as a rookie shows up, there's an older firefighter showing the rookie the ropes. I've seen it happen.

That doesn't mean the rest of the firefighters can slack off. We should all take every opportunity we see to pass on information to the younger generation. It should be a badge of success for us, as the older generation of leaders, if the younger kids grow up to be successful firefighters. As a matter of fact, each generation should be more successful than the last.

If you've done your job well, then you can go to a conference and leave your department behind without being worried. If you're worried that the firehouse will be burned down when you come home, then you probably haven't been a very good mentor.

We even use mentoring in other areas of our work. For example, when we teach at conferences, we do a two-day hands-on program. Some days we have other classes to teach on a variety of topics. In those cases, we have our number two people in our teaching lives, too.

They've been with us forever and we both trust them with the program. Curtis was my stoker at the University of Illinois around twenty years ago. We've crawled down the same hallways dozens of times, and now we teach together.

Chris was John's firefighter a few years back (I won't say how many), and he runs the show for him as well. So we've both worked with these guys for years and we trust them with the programs we've built. As long as the phone doesn't start ringing off the hook, then we know the show is running smoothly. We trained them well so we can be confident in their abilities. It's that simple.

SIGN OF A SUCCESSFUL MENTOR

Do you know what is the surest sign you've been a good mentor? The person you mentored doesn't need you. If you left that job tomorrow, that person wouldn't freak out and say, "Oh my God! What are we going to do now? The chief is gone! Nobody knows how to run this place like the chief."

If everything just flowed smoothly and nobody missed a beat, then you've done your job well. Everyone was ready to step into their role at the next level. You did all you had to in order to prepare the next generation. That's how you know you're a successful mentor.

No matter how high up the chain of command you get, don't think that you know everything. Sharing information goes both ways. You need to learn to listen as well as teach. You have to remind yourself, "Nothing I say today will teach me a thing." You already know everything you're going to say, so shut up and try to learn something! That's why God gave you *one* mouth and *two* ears. Listen twice as much as you talk.

15
WHAT KIND OF LEADER ARE YOU?

As a leader—as it is with pretty much anything you do in life—you have to constantly assess just how effective you are, and how passionate you are about what it is you are doing. In order to do this effectively you have to be able to identify your strengths and weaknesses and then work on how you can improve with both. So many leaders spend so much time on trying to improve their weaknesses and fixing those failures that they forget to spend time on their strengths as well. They hear so much about focusing on fixing things, building those weaknesses into strengths, that they pay no attention to the successes they have enjoyed and the reasons for those successes. Their strengths weaken, and become just one more area to fix.

Good leaders have the ability to look at themselves and evaluate just how much of an impact they are having on those who work for them and with them, and just what kind of a job they are doing for the people they work for. Conversely, *great* leaders have the ability to do the above, but as they do, truly do evaluate what they are they doing, and how they are doing it. It's one thing to believe what's in your own "newspaper clippings," but it's another to look hard at yourself in the mirror and be able to say to yourself that something's not working, or I need to improve on this or that.

Often it's our egos that interfere and block us from being honest with just how well we are performing, especially as leaders. We want to do well, we want to make a difference, but thinking that we are weak in an area or not performing as well as we think we should gets all clogged up when our voices on the inside begin to tell us we're doing a great job and that we know everything that is needed for you to be successful, when in reality we know that could never be and that we are or should be in a constant state of learning. Never halt the learning process, for when you do, you begin to feel the sting of mediocrity.

*Good leaders have the ability to look at themselves
and evaluate just how much of an impact they are
having on those who work for them with them,
and just what kind of a job they are doing
for the people they work for.*

So what kind of a leader are you? Throughout the previous chapters in this book we have been discussing the traits of a good leader and the methods and means for getting becoming one. But how do you know? How do you evaluate just how well you are leading? It takes being honest and it takes the willingness to ask others, your mentors, bosses, and, yes, your subordinates, just how well you are doing.

*Never halt the learning process, for when you do,
you begin to feel the sting of mediocrity.*

ASKING YOUR SUBORDINATES

There are many who feel that if you ask the people who work for you how you are doing that it shows a sign of weakness, a lack of confidence, or a "I don't know what I'm doing" kind of image. Actually, it does quite the opposite! Leaders who are willing to let their people know that they are concerned about how well *they* (the leaders) are doing, asking if they are meeting the needs of the team, or are they missing something, often show a sign of strength and confidence. Leaders who can do that more often than not display even more confidence, which the team can feed off of. No one wants to work for a know-it-all, but they do want to work for people who know what they are doing,and who have their best interest at heart. You can't get there if your only concern is for yourself; and worse yet, if you are constantly telling yourself that you're doing fine and need no improvements. There is always room for and a genuine need for self-improvement.

Again, the positive side of doing this is that your people will know that you truly do care; the negative side can be doing it too often. There needs to be a balance of when, how often, and an understanding that it's all about timing. A leader going there too often can appear to lack confidence, if every time you do something, every time you make a decision, you ask, "How did I do?" There's a big difference between asking your subordinates what they think every time you make a decision and asking them about a particular project, or every now and then, how you are doing as their leader.

ASKING YOUR BOSSES

Every now and then you have to have the nerve to sit down with your boss and ask how you are doing. Are you meeting expectations, doing what is needed, and are there any areas that need improvement? So many leaders have difficulty here, because they fear that if they do this it will show a sign of weakness to their boss, and he or she will start looking for someone else to do their job. For starters, if your boss is any kind of a good leader, they he or she will appreciate this and look at it as a sign of confidence, a positive means of communication. This kind of relationship many times will confirm that the decision to hire or promote you was the right one. It also helps bosses by taking away that uneasy feeling that most leaders have when trying not to offend someone by mentioning a particular weakness. It can be a tension or pressure reducer, and makes for a much more comfortable process. This in itself has a way of building more confidence within the team.

ASKING A MENTOR

Probably the best way to evaluate just how you are doing as a leader is to ask a mentor. If that person is a good leader, he or she will be honest with you and offer you the means, tools, and/or solutions for improvement. Besides, unlike a "buddy," it's a lot easier for a mentor to remain objective. The problem with asking a friend is that in most cases you will be told what you *want to hear* instead of what you *need to hear* in an effort not to hurt your feelings or place a strain on your relationship. Good mentors will explain to you that you are doing a good or great job and, when needed, help you identify a weakness or area for improvement, and not sugarcoat anything. They can remain objective because they have that leadership trait of objectiveness already and know that in their own world they needed a nudge or two from mentors when it came to their own self-improvement.

Good mentors will explain to you that you are doing a good or great job and, when needed, will help you identify a weakness or area for improvement, and not sugarcoat anything.

LAND MINES TO AVOID

No one wants to become that leader people don't want to work for. We've all been there, with the boss who makes you feel miserable, unwelcome, or unappreciated. We can remember a time when we felt that way, when we had a boss we hated working for, finding ourselves in a position where we didn't have the passion for the job anymore. The biggest challenge for *us* was to understand that *we* were allowing *ourselves* to feel that way. That as bad as the boss was, we were letting the demon in. That we were choosing to have that attitude and allowing the enemy to win. Remember, the only thing in life that you have absolute control over is your attitude!

As bad as it was though, we finally came to a point where we realized that what we were going through or went through was actually a gift. That we were shown how *not* to be, how *not* to lead, and given a lesson that no classroom could ever offer. Once you take on a viewpoint that you are going to "get over it" as quickly as you can and learn from it, take that lesson and use it for being a better leader, then you have won!

Here are brief descriptions of some of those common land mines, and a few hints on how to avoid stepping on them:

- Understanding that the respect needed by a leader is not commanded or demanded, but instead earned. A good leader realizes early on that respect is a two-way street. You have to show it if you expect to get it (fig. 15–1). If you think that it just appears one day when you become the boss, then you are in for a really tough time. It's a process that should have started a long time ago.

Fig. 15–1. Lewisville (TX) Battalion Chief Jerry Wells, an excellent example of *earned respect*. Chief Wells always has the best interest of his people at heart; he's their leader no doubt, but his people come first—a trait he most likely learned from his father, a very well respected retired Dallas (TX) battalion chief.

- Staying objective and making good decisions. As a leader, you have to constantly stand guard against making hasty or emotional decisions (fig. 15–2). When you fail to take the time to make the right decision—understanding that at emergencies, quick decisions and quick actions are often needed—you often regret the action you took.

Have you ever wished you could grab the words that just came out of your mouth and shove them back in, wishing you had never said them in the first place? What you say in a heated moment can haunt you for years. Then again, if you only think with your heart, then you'll be setting yourself up for issues later on down the road. The key is to never make decisions based on what's solely in your heart. When you do that you become a *subjective* leader. It makes it difficult to render decisions on performance, discipline, and all sorts of other things if you can't keep a clear, *objective* mind. Somewhere in the process, common sense has to enter the picture. The key is connecting the two, *your heart and the common sense side*. Your heart will keep you honest. It will let you know when you're doing something wrong and can serve as that "integrity" guide rope. The common sense side keeps you realistic and grounded, and connecting the two together allows for you to become an objective leader. With it comes fewer issues and a foundation for more success overall.

What you say in a heated moment seconds can haunt you for years.

Fig. 15–2. Leaders who remain calm in spite of an extremely stressful situation makes the right decisions because they don't let the emotion of the moment cloud their judgment.

- Be a mentor. Teach someone, share something with someone—be there for someone! This is an area that slowly started to disappear from the leadership styles of so many good people. In today's world of technology, we've become so dependent on computers, software programs, and the Internet, that we've forgotten one very important part of being a leader: that it takes a human being, a real person, to coach, counsel, and train. You have to actually push in the keyboard, turn around, and face the person who needs help or guidance. There is no software or website that can substitute for being a good mentor. You have to talk to them, work with them, and provide that one-on-one contact that is needed to truly be a mentor. Become a teacher!

- Build those relationships. Good leaders have the ability to build relationships with those who work for them. By doing so they find that it's a lot easier to face issues and challenges if they have an understanding of what makes people tick in the first place. Good leaders need to know where the strengths and weaknesses are; their team's likes and dislikes; where they may be challenged; just how far they can be pushed before breaking under a load or stressor; and where they see themselves within the organization, in the future, and their roles in its success. Get to know your team.

- As a leader, you need to stay interested, involved, and engaged (fig. 15–3). When you become uninterested, the troops can see it like a big blinking red clown nose and may think you don't care about them or that they're not important. Usually, comes the following reputation of being lazy, and one of those company officers no one wants to work for. Is that the kind of image you want to leave them with? If they were to describe you to another person what would they say? Could you take hearing it? Hopefully the answer is *yes*!

"Be here now!"

—*Jerry Wells*

Fig. 15–3. The company officer who is interested, involved, and engaged with the operation, his crew, and the job grabs hold of his crew's interest in both the firehouse and on the fireground.

- When a leader finds himself or herself in that uninterested, disengaged state of mind, often accompanying this is an appearance of being disorganized, lost, or "flying by the seat of your pants." As stated earlier, leaders have to stay interested and engaged in the operation. They need to stay current, fresh, and involved. Train every day, read something about this profession every day, become a student of the fire service.

- Lead with fairness and firmness. Good leaders have the ability to be fair, realistic, and objective in their assignments, decision making, discipline, coaching, and counseling.

  Good leaders have the ability to be fair, but at the same time, firm. Leaders who are "wishy-washy," or who sit on the fence when it comes to their decisions, are viewed as being weak by their subordinates. They soon after realizing this began to doubt every decision they make, even when it may be the right one in the first place. They begin to lack confidence their ability. When this begins to happen, bad times are just around the corner. Understand though, there is a difference between leaders who are fair in their decisions and those who use the "scorched-earth" method of discipline and/or who over-react. In the latter case, leaders tend to punish everyone for what just happened, instead of those responsible, kind of like the high school coach who makes everybody do 50 push-ups because one or two players messed up. That kind of peer pressure doesn't work in the "grown up" world. All it brings with it is resentment by those who have been busting their hump for you and doing a good job, only to be punished because someone else screwed up. All this does is bring with it a frustration that is felt by all, especially by those who have been working hard and doing what's right.

Good leaders have the ability to be fair, realistic, and objective in their assignments, decision making, discipline, coaching, and counseling.

- Avoid being the paranoid leader. This negative trait is usually a result of someone who has something to hide. Paranoid leaders are usual-ly that way for a very good reason. They don't trust anyone, often don't want to hear or move on suggestions other than their own and always need to be out in front when the bosses are around. No matter how hard you try to align with them, show them that you want to be dependable and loyal, they push you away for fear that you'll gain an advantage or be more well liked. It's kind of back to that trust area again: if you're going to lead, and lead well, you need to trust your people.

- Going from buddy to boss. So many firefighters—when making that first leap to that first grade company officer position—have difficul-ty cutting the strings, if you will. For years, you've been a buddy on shift or in the firehouse. You've always been able to kick back and cut up with the guys, and at times, say maybe not the nicest things about your administration or your officers. Well now that has changed, and with that new position comes a certain level of responsibility and its own weight for your shoulders. No one likes a whiner, complainer, blamer, or pot stirrer, and it's a whole lot worse if it's the officer who is the culprit. No one wants to work in a negative place, where they think they're not appreciated by their boss, or where every time they come to work they have to "feel-out" the mood of the person running the show that day. A lot of what we're discussing here connects to the point above about being *objective* rather than *subjective*. What we really need both in the firehouse and out is a leader who makes decisions because they're right and not because they're popular. First and foremost, popular decisions can get you hurt, while good decisions, the right decisions, objective decisions, can keep you safe and out of trouble. Firefighters *do not* want to work for a weak leader, and a "buddy" can easily fall into that trap. Firefighters want to be led! We need more leaders in the firehouse, those who will step up and lead from the front!

- A leader who is dishonest and who can't be trusted is about as effective as leader as water is in your gas tank. No one, and we mean no one, wants to be led by someone who can't be trusted.

No one, and we mean no one, wants to be led by someone who can't be trusted.

The problem is, when you work for leaders who can't be trusted, you never know when they truly have your best interest at heart and when they don't. It's kind of like the bosses who talk about other people negatively, leaving you to wonder what they're saying about you when you're not around. When facing a difficult situation, will they throw you under the bus, or leave you hanging. Bottom line is, if you can't trust them in the firehouse, you can't trust them on the fireground, and that's a bad thing. People who have no integrity, who are dishonest and can't be trusted, will leave you behind when faced with the decision of it's either you or them. They will choose "them" every time. A true leader, a true brother or sister, will *never* leave a buddy behind.

- As was discussed regarding leading with *fairness* and *firmness*, a leader who has no flexibility, who only sees things in black and white, will soon be painted into a corner when trying to make a decision that is fair to those involved. Hey, the rules are the rules, SOPs are just that, but a leader has to have some built in flexibility when assessing each situation and when making decisions. Obviously there is no flexibility when it comes to firefighter safety and with certain rules that are there for obvious reasons, but a leader who tries to rule in the black and white world soon finds out that with just a little bit of understanding, a little bit of "empathy," good, fair, and objective decisions tend to come a lot more easily and with a whole lot less stress. Take in the whole situation, try to see the whole picture, and you'll often find are there are many more options and solutions to what you're dealing with than you ever imagined.

- As you move further down your leadership path, one very common challenge tends to pop up from time to time, and that's being able to let go. This happens a lot with those great firefighters who did everything and always jumped up and took on the project or assignment, which was good, but now as they move to the next level they need to pass the baton to the next person in line. A good leader needs to help the next person be *that* firefighter and be empowered to have the same ownership.

  You have a whole new set of responsibilities and tasks ahead of you at your new level, those that pertain to your position. Try not to be too "hands-on-ish."

- As was discussed in the mentoring section of this book, a leader who lacks a method of *confidentiality* loses the *confidence* of the troops. When they feel that they can no longer go to you, trust you with a professional or personal problem or issue, everyone loses. As a leader you should be at a point in your life where people shouldn't have to tell you "please keep this between you and me." If you're any kind of a leader, you can decide for yourself just what you can discuss and what you can't. You know what you can repeat and what you can't and if you're ever not sure, don't say anything!

A good leader needs to help the next person be that firefighter and be empowered to have the same ownership.

• Along with fairness, objectivity, flexibility, humility, and empathy comes the ability to accept someone's best efforts. We as leaders tend to forget that we were all there at one time. We all needed a little help, in some case, a lot of help, and we all needed that nudge every now and then. All too often, leaders get to a level where they place unrealistic expectations on their people, only to find later that many are failing to accomplish the mission, and now it's difficult to back out and regroup. By the way, there is nothing wrong with backing out and trying a different direction when something isn't working. Don't "stubborn" yourself into a bad situation. Someone accepted your best efforts at one time. You hit the curb the first time you drove the engine and didn't back it into the firehouse straight. We all started somewhere, and good leaders need to grab hold of that whole mentoring thing, define the expectations for them, and then provide their troops with the tools and means, a little guidance along the way, for accomplishing the task.

It's never easy being the leader. Leadership comes with its own set of obstacles and challenges. The old saying of "they never said it was going to be easy" is right on when it comes to being the leader. People want to be led.

They want someone who is confident and has their best interests at heart, who makes coming to work enjoyable, and they want to know that they are going to learn something every day. They want to be trusted and they want someone who is going to keep them safe. Someone who will have their backs in the firehouse and out, and someone who is going to help them grow.

> "A leader may never know where his influence stops."

We all remember that school teacher who made the difference for us when we were young, the one who changed and affected our lives forever. What kind of a leader do you want to be? Who are you going to help? Whose life do you want to impact? Be that leader!

16
IT'S YOUR TIME TO LEAD

As we start to wrap things up here, we want to give you a few points to ponder so you can get a good head start in whatever leadership role you are in, or planning for. Being a leader in the fire service is an important and influential role. Make sure whatever actions you take, whatever statements and decisions you make, never have a negative impact on your outfit. Whether you are a company officer talking to other officers about events that have occurred in your company, or whether you are a chief talking to a news reporter after a fire, always project a positive image of your company or department. Even if things are not going so well right now, even if there are "issues" that need to be addressed within your unit, you should always strive to promote the positive, and protect the reputation and members of your unit.

Never walk past a mistake! As Colin Powell stated in his most recent book, there are several reasons for this important rule. First, when an officer corrects a mistake, it shows that this officer is paying attention to the work that is going on around them and that the organization has standards that need to be met.

"Never walk past a mistake!"

—*Colin Powell*

Second, it shows that the officer has the moral courage to step in and correct a mistake or error committed by his or her subordinates. Third, it shows the firefighters that their leader cares enough about them and the company to make sure they are performing their tasks and assignments correctly—and safely. Fourth, an officer who corrects his or her firefighters, when required, also sets an example for other less senior or aspiring officers that this is the proper way to handle these situations. Finally, it keeps mistakes from becoming commonplace; more importantly, it keeps them from becoming the new "right way" to do something. If you see something being done or said that is improper or downright wrong and you say nothing, you have actually said, "Nice job, that's the way to do it!"

> "Be willing to make decisions . . .
> Don't fall victim to what I call the
> ready-aim-aim-aim-aim syndrome."
>
> —*T. Boone Pickens*

As a leader, you are never going to make everyone happy. It just can't be done. No matter what the issue is and no matter who the firefighters and officers involved are, if you make a decision or issue a directive, some of the people involved will cheer and others will protest. When leaders make decisions based on how they will be received by their followers or subordinates, they are marching down the wrong road. Every decision a fire officer makes, whether it is what firefighter is assigned what position for the shift, or when the company will go out to inspect buildings or hydrants, it must be based on the priorities and standards of the officer and the department. Sure, you can adjust or consider the issues that the firefighters have—which shows that you value their participation and want to try to consider their issues or view of what is going on—but in the end, your decisions and actions must always give priority to the needs of the company or department.

Building relationships builds confidence. As the years go by in our fire service experience, we all meet new people and establish new relationships. Some of the people we meet are colleagues or co-workers, some are supervisors or officers, and some are instructors or trainers. As time goes by, we become closer with some of these folks, and with others we simply maintain a "professional" or casual relationship (fig. 16–1). Some of your friends may get promoted and move on to other assignments within the department or elsewhere; others might move up through the ranks along with you, and work in a nearby unit. As these relationships develop and mature, we realize that we now have many of these people available to us as mentors, advisors, and role models. Imagine for a moment you are a fifteen-year veteran in your department, and two years ago you were promoted to lieutenant. You are now enjoying working in an active company, but there are some personnel issues that need your attention. You have some experience, but you don't feel totally ready to handle these problems by yourself. Well, luckily for you, one of your closest friends on the job was promoted to officer several years ahead of you. Your former captain, who you became close with during your assignment in his company, is now a battalion chief and one of your mentors and role models. Take advantage of these relationships and talk with these officers about your situation to get their advice on how you can most effectively handle the situation. Your professional relationships can have a tremendous positive effect on your confidence as a leader and an officer.

Every decision a fire officer makes,
whether it is what firefighter is assigned
what position for the shift, or when the company
will go out to inspect buildings or hydrants,
must be based on the priorities and standards
of the officer and the department.

Fig. 16–1. Over the years, those relationships grow as we climb that ladder of responsibility. Pictured are FDNY Lt. Mike Wilbur L27 and Captain Joe Principio L58.

Remember what "open-door" really means. We've all heard the term, "I have an open door policy," but do you really know what that means? When we talk about the open door we are simply telling our people that they can come to us at any time with a problem or issue. A good leader—one who cares about his or her people—should always welcome a phone call or even a visit from anyone who needs help or advice. On duty, off duty, day or night, one of your firefighters or officers may turn to you with a difficult job-related or personal issue. If you truly have an open door, your people would not hesitate to come to you for help. What greater display of respect and confidence can a firefighter show than to turn to the company officer for advice, or help? When you decide to move into a leadership role in the fire service and become an officer, you are also moving into a position where you need to consider that your firefighters and fellow officers may ask even more of you than supervising a roll call or fighting a fire.

Stay in touch with the troops. Some great fire officers who are successful and safe and train constantly drop the ball when it comes to staying in touch with their people. This is true for leaders at every level, from company officer to chief of department. We have all heard stories about the company officer who comes in for a shift and has a cup of coffee in the kitchen with the firefighters before retiring to the second floor officer for the next five hours. Or the story about the chief of a midsized department who stops by a firehouse and tells the firefighter who answers the door that he will be parking his private vehicle in their parking lot for a few hours. When the young firefighters ask who he is, the chief explodes and screams that he is the chief of department, and the firefighter should know that. Well, the lieutenant who hides up in the office and the chief who doesn't make it his business to visit the fire stations regularly are not staying in touch with their troops. This also creates a situation where they lose touch with the people that they are responsible for, and don't notice any of the issues or problems that are developing. An officer who does not walk around the firehouse, stop by the TV room, visit the kitchen or sit in the house watch area with the firefighters, now and then, is out of touch and much less able to uncover or deal with the many firehouse issues that are certainly going on daily.

Define your expectations. This is an important component of a good roll call for a company officer, and for any leader in any assignment in a fire department. Whether you are working in the fire prevention office or a rescue company, you need to get your people together and let them know what is expected of them. A company officer in the field should start the shift with a quick rundown of the items or events he or she would like to get accomplished during the tour. Obviously, we are not spelling out every minute of every day, but letting everyone know what's planned helps them adjust or change their plans.

*Whether you are working in the
fire prevention office or a rescue company,
you need to get your people together and let
them know what is expected of them.*

Another aspect of expectations relates to conduct and behavior. After just a few shifts at a new assignment, a firefighter should have been told or instructed or simply shown "how we do things around here." Each shift and company has its own habits and standards, and as a leader, you need to make sure that every firefighter on your shift, whether there for the day or for years, knows what is expected. A good leader sets the standard and a good crew will surely rise to the occasion.

Don't be afraid to try new things. Can you imagine what the world would be like if we never tried anything new? I remember when I was working as a firefighter in Rescue 3 in the Bronx and our lieutenant brought in one of the first "Rabbit" tools for us to check out. The first few runs we went on, the bag with the tool was thrown out the back door as we pulled out of the firehouse; needless to say, the tool was not going over very big. After a few days, we did take it to a few jobs, but didn't use it, and finally a couple of guys did carry it up and try it out. It worked so well and so quickly that in a short period of time, truck companies were asking for it to be brought up to the fire floor. Today, every truck, squad, and rescue company in the FDNY carries a hydraulic forcible entry tool, as do hundreds of companies in fire departments throughout the nation. I'm sure glad we tried something new.

Make decisions on good solid information and common sense, not on emotions. Fire officers and leaders are required to make decisions all the time. Many of these decisions are tactical ones at fires and emergencies, others are administrative or personnel issues (fig. 16–2). If you let your emotions impact your decisions you will almost certainly start making bad or improper decisions. Solid information is facts or knowledge. The old adage "facts before acts" applies here, and those in leadership roles needs to work hard to eliminate their emotions from their decisions. Discipline, in particular, should never be applied by an angry officer. If the infraction or behavior results in you being angry, really mad at the violator, take whatever action is needed to stop the infraction and inform the violator that you will deal with this issue in a day or two. Applying discipline when you are angry will often result in a more serious than necessary or overblown penalty.

Wherever you are in your leadership role, it is important that you realize that leaders and followers, officers and firefighters, are dynamic groups. No two firefighters are going to respond or react to your leadership style the same way. No two officers are going to manage or lead their firefighters in exactly same way. There are many areas that are handled differently by company officers and chiefs, and many of them are doing a great job. There are two great aspects of leadership that make it one of the most important skills a fire officer can possess. First is the fact that leadership is an enhancer. An officer with good or great leadership skills does everything else better. Leadership enhances supervision, fireground safety, training, public education, and recruitment and retention of firefighters. Good leadership skills help you do everything better!

Fig. 16–2. Many times, the leader wishes that the only decisions that had to be made were those at an emergency incident. Administrative and personnel decisions can be the toughest.

*An officer with good or great leadership skills
does everything else better.*

The second aspect of good leadership is that every leader, every officer, every chief can and should perform and practice leadership his or her own way. Each one of us had different adults involved in raising us. We had different teachers, football coaches, scout leaders, and bosses; each of these people contributed to our leadership development along with, and in conjunction with, all of the others. There is no other similar or exact combination of life experiences, training, successes, and failures as yours. Use your common sense, your education, your experience, and your heart to lead your people into the fire and safely home.

ABOUT THE AUTHORS

Chief (ret.) Rick Lasky, a 34-year veteran of the fire service, served as chief of the Lewisville (TX) Fire Department for 12 years. Rick followed in his father's footsteps, beginning his career as a firefighter in the suburbs on the southwest side of Chicago and has been a line firefighter, firefighter-paramedic, company grade officer, training officer, and command-level officer.

While in Illinois, he received the 1996 International Society of Fire Service Instructors "Innovator of the Year" award for his part in developing "Saving Our Own," a program designed to teach firefighters how to save firefighters who have become trapped or lost in a burning building. Rick is a long-standing editorial advisory board member for *Fire Engineering* magazine and as an author has written more than 250 technical articles that have been published in national fire rescue journals. These magazine articles relate to fire department operations, administration, training, and safety. He is the author of the best-selling book *Pride and Ownership: A Firefighter's Love of the Job*, published by Fire Engineering Books, and is the cohost for the radio show *The Command Post* heard on Fire Engineering Talk Radio.

Rick has also served as a police officer, and was wounded on several occasions, once while defending a victim of family violence, and has received numerous fire and police awards and commendations. Rick holds an AAS degree in fire science from Columbia Southern University (CSU), and was selected as the CSU 2012 Distance Education and Training Council (DETC) Outstanding Graduate. He was also honored in 2012 as an inductee into the "Chicago 16" Softball Hall of Fame. He is a Lewisville Honorary Police Officer and Honorary Battalion Commander in the 18th Battalion of the FDNY.

Rick lectures at the local, state, national, and international levels and is a sought-after speaker by both the public and private sectors. A very popular speaker on leadership topics, he has been requested by several businesses and corporations to deliver his inspiring and meaningful leadership development programs. He is married to his best friend, Jami, and they have two children, Rick, a Fleet Marine Force Navy corpsman, and Emily, an outstanding fast-pitch softball player.

Battalion Chief (ret.) John Salka has served 33 years with the New York Fire Department (FDNY) and has held assignments in some of the department's most active and specialized units. In addition to his many years of engine and ladder company duties, Chief Salka has worked in several units of the FDNY special operations command. As a firefighter, after receiving two department medals for meritorious acts, he was transferred to Rescue Company 3 in upper Manhattan where he worked for several years with that specialized unit operating at working fires, building collapses, confined space events, and numerous other technical rescue operations in Manhattan, Harlem, and the Bronx. He was promoted to lieutenant from there and attended the First Line Supervisors Training School at the FDNY Academy, returning to the field as a company officer. Shortly thereafter, he was recruited to join the newly formed FDNY Special Operations Command, where he performed duty in the busy squad and rescue companies throughout the five boroughs of New York City until his assignment to Squad 1 in Brooklyn. Chief Salka served several years in the squad until his promotion to captain, which brought him a new assignment as a company commander in the Bronx at Engine 48. The next promotion was to battalion chief, and Chief Salka quickly secured a spot in the busy 18th Battalion in the central Bronx, where he served for more than 15 years, attaining the designation battalion commander.

Chief Salka's training experience includes work with numerous public and private organizations including the FDNY, colleges and universities, fortune 500 companies, and the US military. As a lieutenant, Salka was an instructor at the FDNY Probationary Firefighter's School; as a captain he instructed at the Captains' Management Program, and for several years, as a battalion chief, he was on the staff of the Battalion Chiefs' Command Course. Chief Salka has served as a program developer for the FDNY and the NY State Office of Fire Prevention and Control and has delivered both classroom training and hands-on programs for Firehouse Expo in Baltimore and the Fire Department Instructors Conference (FDIC) in Indianapolis.

Chief Salka is the author of two books, *First In, Last Out: Leadership Lessons From the New York Fire Department,* which was published in 2004 and is used throughout the country for company officer test preparation and for college leadership courses, and *The Engine Company*, published in 2009 by Fire Engineering Books. In addition to his books, Chief Salka writes the back page monthly column in *Firehouse* magazine, "The Fire Scene," and has written numerous technical articles for *Fire Engineering, Size-Up*, and the FDNY training magazine *WNYF (With New York Firefighters)*.